THE GOOD NEWS OF THE KINGDOM

WHAT IT MEANS TO BECOME A CHRISTIAN

THE GOOD NEWS OF THE KINGDOM

WHAT IT MEANS TO BECOME A CHRISTIAN

BOB SANTOS

SEARCH FOR ME MINISTRIES, INC.
INDIANA, PA

The Good News of the Kingdom: Understanding What It Means to Become a Christian
By Bob Santos

Copyright © 2025 by Search for Me Ministries, Inc.
First Edition

Cover Design: Path & Paper

Unless otherwise indicated, Scripture quotations are taken from the 1995 version of the New American Standard Bible®, Copyright © 1960, 1971, 1977, 1995 by The Lockman Foundation. All rights reserved.

Scripture quotations marked (HCSB) are taken from the Holman Christian Standard Bible®. Used by Permission HCSB ©1999, 2000, 2002, 2003, 2009 Holman Bible Publishers. Holman Christian Standard Bible®, Holman CSB®, and HCSB® are federally registered trademarks of Holman Bible Publishers.

Published by SfMe Media
Indiana, PA 15701
www.sfme.org

Printed in the United States of America

Library of Congress Control Number: 2025934157

ISBN: 978-1-937956-37-0
EPUB ISBN: 978-1-937956-38-7

CONTENTS

Introduction	7
1. What Is the Good News?	9
2. The Bible	15
3. Who Is God?	21
4. Creation	29
5. The Crash	35
6. Laws of the Kingdom	41
7. Taking the Path of Grace	47
8. Wise Compassion	53
9. Setting the Record Straight	59
10. The Redemptive Power of the Cross	65
11. An Eye on the Veil	71
12. Born Anew	77
13. With Open Eyes	83
14. Water Baptism	89
15. A New Identity	95
16. Free!	101
17. The Gift of the Holy Spirit	107
18. Communion	113
19. Why So Many Denominations?	119
20. Connected	125
21. The Dynamics of Forgiveness	131
22. Manna from Heaven	137
23. The Gift of Prayer	143
24. The End Is the Beginning	149
25. Resurrection Life!	155
Conclusion	161

Introduction

One recent morning, I had a "moment." Our church was in the middle of a three-week morning prayer initiative to begin the year. Thirty or forty devoted souls would brave well-below-freezing temps to gather at 7:00 sharp for worship, a short message, and group prayer. I participated in several of those meetings despite not being a morning person. Do not get me wrong, I love mornings, but would function a whole lot better if they came later in the day.

During a time of worship, I thought to myself, "I can't believe I'm doing this. The whole idea of Jesus and Christianity seems so crazy at times." I mean, we are talking about some bizarre—from a human perspective—ideas. To think that an eternal God created everything, when so many scientific authorities proclaim a different story. What about the concept of the Trinity—the idea that God is Three in One? And certainly more than one person has struggled to comprehend how God could—or would—step down from the glories of heaven to become a human destined for a torturous death through crucifixion.

Having been a follower of Christ for more than four decades, and involved in ministry as a vocation for over half that time, I was not experiencing a crisis of faith. For me, it was more a time to marvel at the unlikely course taken by this self-professed science nerd.

Three primary reasons highlight my continued devotion to God, while three primary "holes" in evolutionary theory cause me to question the lofty claims of scientific naturalists (i.e., atheists).

First, having spent a lifetime seeking a deeper understanding of who God is and how the Christian life works, the teachings of the Bible ring true. I cannot say all my questions have been answered; some never will be in this life. But the deeper I dig, the more "treasure" I find. Second, I have seen the transformational influence of heaven's wisdom on human lives, beginning with my own. When rightly understood and applied, Biblical principles welcome divine blessings to our lives and the world around us. Third, I have experienced the presence of God innumerable times and in untold ways. I am not talking about simply living a life based on principles, but one in which an active relationship with our eternal Creator stands at the center of my existence.

When considering scientific naturalism, I find unanswered questions of an enormous magnitude. To begin, we continue to learn that the expanse of our universe reaches far beyond our ability to grasp. How did it all come into existence? Why do we have something instead of nothing? Evolutionary biologists will tell us that is not their field of study, but whose is it? What scientific authority can even begin to explain the existence of our cosmos in a scientifically credible way?

Scientists also struggle to explain the existence of life. The Miller-Urey experiments of the early 1950s seemed to point to an answer. Grant monies flowed, and well-designed experiments were conducted, but the trail soon went cold. I continue to see many speculative statements regarding the origin of life, but none have substance.

Finally, how can we begin to fathom the profound complexity of our human bodies? How do we explain human consciousness? What about the conscience? Each of us is born with an internal moral compass. The needle might be pointed in a skewed direction, but it exists nonetheless. And the complexity of human DNA is off the charts—at least from an evolutionary perspective.

More than *ten billion miles of DNA* in your body speak of *intention* and *purpose*. You are not here because of a mindless accident or random process. Meaning can be found only through the God who created you. Discovering purpose and meaning, however, require intentional effort because we do not naturally align with our Creator's ways.

And so it is that I present *The Good News of the Kingdom*. Some might take offense to the ideas within, but more than anything, this book provides a message of hope amid a seemingly hopeless existence.

Heaven's King is good in every way, and He ever desires the best for each of us. But we play a vital role in positioning ourselves to align with the kingdom of heaven. If you will read intently, process the contents of this book thoughtfully, and align your life with God's kingdom prayerfully, you will be amazed by the depths of goodness the Lord extends in your direction.

Chapter 1

What Is the Good News?

Have you ever had a bad experience with a government agency? Probably. Have you ever been adversely affected by a government policy? I am sure you have. Have you ever heard a negative news report about a corrupt government official? Pretty much all the time!

In principle, governments are good and necessary, passing laws and maintaining infrastructure for the well-being of a community, state, or nation. But in practice, politicians and their governments routinely fall short of their noble proclamations.

Not surprisingly, the people of Jesus' day were unhappy with the dynamics of their government. The once-mighty nation of Israel had squandered its God-given sovereignty, and so its citizens struggled under the oppressive rule of the Roman Empire. To compound the misery, many Jewish leaders had fallen prey to the allure of power and greed. Public devotion to God only poorly masked the toxic motives bubbling from their polluted hearts. In the name of pious religion, Pharisees, Sadducees, and scribes were enriching themselves by exploiting the masses. Is that not what corrupt leaders do—enrich their pockets and inflate their egos at the expense of those they lead?

JESUS CHRIST

It was in such an environment that the angel Gabriel visited a young virgin named Mary with the strangest of announcements: she would miraculously give birth to the long-awaited *Messiah*—a descendant of the revered King David:

> "He will be great and will be called the Son of the Most High; and the Lord God will give Him the throne of His father David; and He will reign over the house of Jacob forever, and His

> kingdom will have no end . . . . The Holy Spirit will come upon you, and the power of the Most High will overshadow you; and for that reason the holy Child shall be called the Son of God." Luke 1:32–33, 35b

The coming kingdom proclaimed by the angel would prove vastly different from everyone's expectations—the reality of which became apparent when Jesus was born in a barn-like area and His birth announced to lowly shepherds.

When He was about thirty years old, having been preceded by John the Baptist, Jesus went public with His ministry efforts by preaching "the gospel of the kingdom":

> Jesus was going throughout all Galilee, teaching in their synagogues and proclaiming the gospel of the kingdom, and healing every kind of disease and every kind of sickness among the people. Matthew 4:23

> Now after John had been taken into custody, Jesus came into Galilee, preaching the gospel of God, and saying, "The time is fulfilled, and the kingdom of God is at hand; repent and believe in the gospel." Mark 1:14–15

The word "gospel" is an English rendering of the Greek *euaggelion* (Latin *evangelium*), which means "good news."[1] And the theme of the good news of the kingdom runs from the Old Testament of the Christian Bible into the New. The message proclaims the glad tidings of a great King who will establish God's benevolent rule on earth. Jesus is that King, and so the four books of the New Testament that tell of His life (Matthew, Mark, Luke, and John) are called "the gospels."

Scholars identify the first three of these books as "synoptic" gospels because they present similar perspectives of Jesus' life, sayings, and ministry—even sharing some of the same content. The Gospel of John takes a somewhat different approach, and so it stands apart in that sense.

---
1. Robert L. Thomas, *New American Standard Hebrew-Aramaic and Greek Dictionaries: Updated Edition* (Anaheim: Foundation Publications, Inc., 1998).

THE KING AND HIS KINGDOM

The kingdom of God reflects the domain of an all-powerful and sovereign King. And while this might not appear to be good news at first glance, the character of this Monarch far surpasses that of every other ruler who has ever existed. Rarely do the actions of politicians and government leaders live up to the noble images they portray, but this King stands at the pinnacle of truth and moral perfection.

People, including leaders, normally function with a "What's in it for me?" mindset. If you look at a group picture, what person grabs your attention first? And if you are waiting in a long line, whose challenged schedule occupies your thoughts? Even people we consider unselfish will often be preoccupied with their needs for tomorrow.

So exactly what is the good news of the kingdom? *There is a King—all-powerful, all-knowing, sovereign, eternal, good, and unselfish—whose kingdom is advancing across the globe. With each piece of ground gained, evil is vanquished and human lives restored. On a day yet to come, His kingdom will be the only one standing.*

In proclaiming the gospel of the kingdom of God, we are not declaring our governments or political systems to be unimportant; they affect so many aspects of our lives. But we are proclaiming the advance of a greater kingdom on earth, and in this we put our hope, regardless of what is going on around us. Our wise and mighty King will one day put an end to injustice, call the unjust into account, and establish a never-ending dominion of peace.

It was for this reason that, on the night Jesus was born in a stable, a glorious angel proclaimed, "Do not be afraid; for behold, I bring you good news of great joy which will be for all the people; for today in the city of David there has been born for you a Savior, who is Christ the Lord" (Luke 2:10b–11).

THE GOOD KING

Jesus lived like no government official born before or after. In Him, we see a lifestyle entirely congruent with His selfless, moral teachings. Jesus came seeking not His own benefit, but the well-being of others. In Christ, we see no quest for political power, no innate cravings for glory and human approval, and no hint of desire for riches and wealth. Jesus sought to heal and restore the downtrodden—never to oppress or exploit. And He did so sacrificially, paying a steep price for the benefit of others. The announcement of a government led by such a King is good news indeed!

As wonderful as the news of God's coming kingdom may be, it does not advance without pain or conflict. Jesus exhorted people to "repent and believe in the gospel" (Mark 1:15). To *repent* means to change one's mindset, to the point of affecting everyday actions. In other words, the kingdom of God runs by a set of laws that conflict with our natural thinking. Some people confuse the kingdom with a form of social justice, but they are trying to create the fruit of repentance without repentance itself. *If we want to be citizens of the Lord's good kingdom, we must change our approach to life at the root level.*

These ideas challenge us, but they mark the difference between a real God and one formed by human design. I have tried to conform our Creator to my imaginations, but find Him not at all pliable in that regard. The King is good and benevolent, but the King is also **the King**—not a pawn to be moved and manipulated at our discretion. The idea of a "god" who is subject to manipulation should terrify us. Perhaps I have read too much history or seen humanity too closely, but I could never embrace a god conceived in our likeness. I might have questions about some of our Creator's actions, but I have experienced His goodness firsthand and cannot imagine choosing any other.

Heaven's King will never craft public policy based on popularity polls. None of its leaders can be threatened, bribed, or coerced. The eternal King does what is right and just and true regardless of how people respond. This, too, is good news. He will not be swayed from righteousness and justice no matter how loud human voices rise.

The news of the kingdom is good because heaven's King is good in every way imaginable. And not only is He good, He is all-powerful. The day will surely come when the Lord crushes evil underfoot and liberates His people from its influence and pain.

Much remains to be said about the good news of God's kingdom, but we must first establish several necessary foundations. In our next chapter, we will consider a basic overview of *the Bible*.

Digging Deeper Into Chapter One

Jesus Christ stands at the center of the Christian faith. Never has there been a person like Jesus to walk this earth. But He did not suddenly appear without warning. Many Old Testament prophecies predicted the coming of Christ, His kingship, and His kingdom.

Dig deeper: Daniel 2:1–45
Isaiah 9:6–7

Because the coming King was prophesied to be of David's lineage (2 Samuel 7:12–13), the people of Israel had fixed their attention on the arrival of a valiant warrior who would break the rule of the Roman Empire over their nation. Jesus created considerable confusion because He did not fit the mold of their expectations.

The story was so good, and Jesus so unique, that four devoted followers felt the need to provide written accounts of His life, death, and resurrection. And though their perspectives vary—as they always do when eyewitness testimony is involved—the core elements of their stories remain the same.

The Gospel of Luke (in addition to the book of Acts) was written by a physician, who also proved to be a detailed historian. The first chapter of Luke's gospel sets the stage for Jesus' birth. Then, in a passage many call "The Christmas Story," Luke records the story of Christ's unique birth.

Dig deeper: Luke 2:1–20

Luke, who was an associate and traveling companion of the apostle Paul, was not the only person to record the good news of the life of Christ. Matthew and John, who were disciples of Jesus, also put the story of His dynamic life to paper. Finally, Mark's gospel likely contains the eyewitness account of Jesus' disciple Peter.

We see in the gospels that Jesus seemed to always keep people off balance. The self-proclaimed "Son of Man" was not trying to make anyone stumble. He simply lived on a higher moral plane, viewing life through a spiritual lens that often conflicted with the natural perspectives of this world.

> Therefore Pilate entered again into the Praetorium, and summoned Jesus and said to Him, "Are You the King of the Jews?" Jesus answered, "Are you saying this on your own initiative, or did others tell you about Me?" Pilate answered, "I am not a Jew, am I? Your own nation and the chief priests delivered You to me; what have You done?" Jesus answered, "My kingdom is not of this world. If My kingdom were of this world, then My servants would be fighting so that I would not be handed over to the Jews; but as it is, My kingdom is not of this realm." John 18:33–36

Becoming a Christian is not about simply adding a new perspective or ideal to a person's life. The Christian life embraces a radically different way of thinking and living—one that aligns with the dynamics of God's eternal kingdom.

The quest before us is one of *discovery* and *alignment*. We begin by seeking God for wisdom to understand His ways. As we learn, we adjust our lives to align with His good design. And as we align, we welcome the presence of our Savior and all that comes with it. I cannot begin to think of anything more meaningful!

QUESTIONS

1. What do you find interesting regarding the Old Testament prophecies about Jesus?
2. What does the Christmas Story tell us about God's intentions?
3. How does Jesus differ from the rulers and leaders of this world?
4. How might the kingdom of God differ from the kingdoms of humanity?
5. What does it mean to repent?
6. How does repentance relate to the process of becoming a Christian?

Chapter 2
The Bible

Modern advances in technology have lessened the burden of life in many ways. I remember well trying to navigate an unfamiliar city using a paper map. And more than once, a cell phone could have saved me grief had I been able to call and tell my wife I was running late after a morning on a trout stream.

Technology also has its drawbacks, and perhaps the greatest is the role it has played in the erosion of trust. People in positions of power have always had a history of lying to the public, but now we can learn of those falsehoods in the blink of an eye. I can also remember an era when society trusted reputable news anchors. Except for network promotional ads, the words "reputable" and "news anchor" are rarely used in the same sentence these days—and there are valid reasons why.

One of our most formidable challenges involves not knowing whom to trust. How many times have we heard a government official provide an "absolute" statement to the public, only to later learn it was a bald-faced lie? We have access to information like never before, but how we struggle to discern the actual truth!

We could say something similar about the various religions and their perspectives of God. The unseen nature of the spiritual world complicates this issue all the more. That is why our gracious Creator has gifted us with the Bible. The Bible defines Christianity, and without it we would be left to our own imaginations.

Hundreds of millions of lives have been transformed through the Christian Scriptures. Entire educational systems have been developed, heinous practices abolished, and the dignity of humanity championed. Yes, we face enormous challenges with injustice and oppression in our world today, but the situation would be far worse if not for the influence of the Bible.

Questions remain, of course. The Bible was completed almost 2,000 years ago, leaving us with a somewhat fragmented picture of the process. It can also be a challenging book to understand, which provides an opportunity for people of bad moral character to exploit others in the name of God. All things considered, though, the Bible serves as an amazing gift from heaven for the benefit of humanity.

Scholars have written thousands of pages about the credibility of the Bible, so I will provide just enough of an overview to build upon.

THE CREDIBILITY OF THE BIBLE

- The Bible was written by forty different authors over a 1,500-year span, and yet its sixty-six books tell a cohesive story. Getting only two people to agree on anything without coercion can sometimes prove challenging, so in the Bible we see evidence of a *single* Author—God Himself.

- The Bible was written within the backdrop of human history. Unlike most religious writings, many of its personalities and geographical locations have been confirmed through the accounts of ancient historians and archaeological discoveries. You can even purchase an *Archaeological Study Bible* that highlights many of the finds.[1]

- The Old Testament contains hundreds of major and minor prophecies fulfilled by Jesus Christ. But Jesus had no control over where He was born, His brief stay in Egypt, the method of His death, and the price paid to Judas for His betrayal. One of the most graphic pictures of Christ's crucifixion comes from Isaiah 53, which was confirmed through the Dead Sea Scrolls to have been written well *before* Christ's birth.

- Because of intense persecution and the fragility of ancient writing materials, we do not have original manuscripts from the Bible. However, scholars can compare thousands of full and partial manuscript copies from varying religious streams.

---

1. *Archaeological Study Bible: An Illustrated Walk Through Biblical History and Culture* (Grand Rapids, MI: Zondervan Publishing House, 2005).

And from a historical perspective, the time span between the actual events and the earliest manuscript copies is relatively short. If we declare the Bible invalid as a historical document, we must also discard much of ancient history as we know it. Our evidence for the Bible is that significant!

- I am touched by the stories of intelligent and inquisitive skeptics who set out to investigate, or even disprove, the story of Christ and become Christians in the process. Men such as Sir William Ramsay (archaeologist), C. S. Lewis (university professor), Lee Strobel (investigative journalist), and J. Warner Wallace (cold-case detective) have written extensively of the experiences that turned their skepticism upside down.

Although the Bible was penned thousands of years ago, we have sufficient evidence to laud it as *credible* and *worthy* of its revered status. Therefore, as Christians, we recognize the Scriptures to be *inspired* by God, *infallible* for His intended purposes, and *authoritative* regarding spiritual and moral issues.

THE CANON OF SCRIPTURE

Some people refer to the Bible as the "canon of Scripture," meaning its sixty-six books establish the *standard* for spiritual truth.

Can you imagine our world without well-defined standards of measurement? How would you know if you got the full value for your purchase of fruit, cereal, or milk? Utility companies could charge whatever they wanted, and it would be anybody's guess whether the amount of gas you purchased would take you safely through a dry, barren landscape. Governments all over the world establish objective standards to ensure the world of commerce is fair and just.

I once worked in the laboratory of a large mining company. We analyzed the quality of the millions of tons of coal bought and sold by our company. Even slight errors could have a significant financial impact, and so we established procedures for every part of the testing process. As each shift began, we calibrated the lab scales according to standardized weights. And when the supervisor of another department asked if we could bias the scales just a little in our company's favor, my response was simple and straightforward: "No, sir! We don't do that kind of thing here. Our job is to provide the most accurate number possible."

By design, commercial standards are *objective*. They never depend upon a CEO's desires, how a store owner feels about a customer, or how much money is owed on a business debt.

Similar principles apply to matters of spirituality. The spiritual realm cannot be seen, but that does not make it unreal. Spiritual issues exert an enormous influence—both physical and eternal—on our lives. But without a credible standard, how could we discern what is true? How would we protect ourselves from error and the unscrupulous efforts of false prophets? And so it is that God, in His goodness, has provided the Bible as *the standard* for spiritual truth.

RECOGNIZING THE BIBLE'S VALUE

In the fall of 1536, an executioner strangled linguistic scholar William Tyndale and burned him at the stake. The terrible crime committed? Though formally accused of heresy, Tyndale had defied church and government officials by translating the Greek and Hebrew Scriptures into the *common tongue*. By keeping people ignorant of the Bible, unscrupulous leaders of church and state had been manipulating and controlling the masses in the name of religion.

Tyndale recognized the value of the Bible and the lengths to which those in power were going to conceal its truths. In an argument with a bishop, he proclaimed, "If God spare my life, ere many years pass, I will cause a boy that driveth the plow [to] know more of the Scripture than thou dost."[2] William Tyndale did indeed lose his life, but his translating efforts became the foundation for the King James version of the Bible, which has touched untold millions.

Today, from the least to the greatest, we can each learn from God through the Christian Scriptures. And though pastors and priests play valuable roles in our efforts to know the Lord and align with His ways, nothing compares to the honor of learning from the Author Himself.

---

2. Dr. Tony Lane, "A Man for All People: Introducing William Tyndale," *Christian History Magazine*, 1987, accessed February 14, 2025, https://christianhistoryinstitute.org/magazine/article/a-man-for-all-people.

Digging Deeper Into Chapter Two

It would likely take a PhD program in religious studies for a person to learn all the beliefs in our world. Throughout history, humans have worshiped thousands of gods. But how do we know what is true?

The Aztecs sacrificed children to their god *Tlaloc* with the hopes of abundant rain and fertility. Who is to say it is wrong to kill innocent children as an offering to the gods? We need a standard for moral and spiritual truth, which is one reason our Creator gave us the Scriptures.

The Bible consists of two primary parts—the *Old Testament* (39 books) and the *New Testament* (27 books)—that work in conjunction with one another.

Finding its roots in the *law of Moses*, the physical elements of the Old Testament help illuminate the eternal spiritual reality of the New Testament. And the New Testament, which centers around the *new covenant* in Christ, both fulfills and supersedes the Old Testament.

The Protestant version of the Old Testament—also known as the *Hebrew Bible*—contains:

- *The Law:* Genesis, Exodus, Leviticus, Numbers, and Deuteronomy (5 books)
- *History:* Joshua, Judges, Ruth, 1 and 2 Samuel, 1 and 2 Kings, 1 and 2 Chronicles, Ezra, Nehemiah, and Esther (12 books)
- *Poetry:* Job, Psalms, Proverbs, Ecclesiastes, and Song of Solomon (5 books)
- *The Major Prophets:* Isaiah, Jeremiah, Lamentations, Ezekiel, and Daniel (5 books)
- *The Minor Prophets:* Hosea, Joel, Amos, Obadiah, Jonah, Micah, Nahum, Habakkuk, Zephaniah, Haggai, Zechariah, and Malachi (12 books)

The New Testament contains:

- *The Gospels:* Matthew, Mark, Luke, and John (4 books)
- *History:* Acts (1 book)
- *Paul's Letters (Epistles):* Romans, 1 and 2 Corinthians, Galatians, Ephesians, Philippians, Colossians, 1 and 2 Thessalonians, 1 and 2 Timothy, Titus, Philemon, and Hebrews (14 books)
- *The General Epistles:* James, 1 and 2 Peter, 1, 2, and 3 John, and Jude (7 books)
- *Prophecy:* Revelation (1 book)

The Bible is *inspired* by God, meaning the Creator of our Universe breathed life into the words He inspired human authors to write.

Dig deeper: 2 Timothy 3:14–17
2 Peter 1:19–21

The Holy Spirit promises to reveal and illuminate the truth of His eternal Word if we will seek with honest and humble hearts.

See also: John 8:31–32
James 1:5–8

William Tyndale was on to something! God desires all people to know Him through His eternal Word. In quoting Deuteronomy 8:3, Jesus once said, "Man shall not live on bread alone, but on every word that proceeds out of the mouth of God" (Matthew 4:4). And so it is!

QUESTIONS

1. How does the Bible provide evidence of a single Author?
2. Why is it significant that the Bible contains genuine history?
3. What vital purposes does the Bible serve?
4. Why do we need a standard for moral and spiritual truth?
5. How does the Old Testament serve the New Testament?
6. Why should "common" people read and study the Bible?

Chapter 3
Who Is God?

"TRUST THE UNIVERSE." "THE UNIVERSE HAS YOUR BACK." "THE UNIVERSE SMILES ON YOU." "SURRENDER TO THE UNIVERSE." These are just a few of the messages I have seen regarding our faltering existence amid an immense cosmos. But what do they mean? How can we trust "THE UNIVERSE" to do what is in our best interests?

From a purely natural perspective, there is nothing for us to trust apart from the physical laws of nature. We can crawl out of bed in the morning and walk across the floor, trusting the earth's gravitational pull to keep us from drifting toward deep space. But regarding our personal interests, the universe does not care. It operates by natural, unguided processes.

We can also view the universe through a spiritual lens, which is the purpose of the quotes above. They reflect a *pantheistic* perspective, which declares that "God is all, and all is God."

"The universe is good and worthy of our trust," we are encouraged to believe. And because we are part of the universe, we each have a "divine spark" within which can be realized only as we learn to believe in and trust ourselves. How do we know these things to be true? "We discover them as we follow the expert guidance of those who have already been enlightened"—or so we are told.

The Bible—our standard for spiritual truth—tells a very different story. It speaks of a world created by a good, sovereign God who exists above and apart from His created order. We are not gods ourselves, but depend upon the one true God for our provision—even the air we breathe.

It is from the Bible—the Book of books—that we learn about the true nature of God and His goodness. Otherwise, we find ourselves visiting a "buffet" of spiritual beliefs with no way of knowing what is nourishing or poisonous. And nothing can be more important than knowing God—the very source of our existence. What we believe about our Creator affects practically every area of life.

We often learn about God in terms of isolated concepts, but He is seamlessly whole. For example, the Lord is both loving and just, with no conflict between the two. So while we find value in analytically separating the various attributes of the Almighty, we must remember that each is part of a greater nonconflicting whole.

UNIFIED

The Bible tells of the Father, Son, and Holy Spirit seamlessly bound together in perfect unity (Matthew 28:19). Each Person of the Trinity (a.k.a. Godhead) plays a different role, but is otherwise identical in nature. The one exception would be that Jesus confined Himself to a physical body as the "Son of Man" (Matthew 8:20). Both fully divine and fully human, Jesus was filled beyond measure with the Holy Spirit.

RELATIONAL

As mysterious as it might seem, from a relational perspective, the concept of the *Trinity* is a pearl of great price. God is not a lone, aloof entity who rules from afar. Father, Son, and Holy Spirit characterize love and relational oneness to the highest degree possible.

Humans are relational creatures because we were created by a relational God. And though this world tempts us to pursue pleasure, fame, and wealth above all, those with insight recognize that relationships matter most. Most importantly, the Lord desires us to be intimate with Him, and from that nearness everything else flows. As much as some of us struggle to form healthy relationships, the Lord and His Word can enable our quest to become reality.

"OMNI"

Our Creator is *omnipotent*, *omniscient*, and *omnipresent*. Those might seem like big, complicated words, but they need not be. The word *omni* simply means "all." And so we are saying God is *all powerful* (Jeremiah

32:17), *all knowing* (1 John 3:20), and *all present* (Psalm 139:1–12). Nothing the Lord wants to do lies beyond His ability. No problem can defy His wisdom and knowledge. And there is nowhere we can go that He is not already present.

SOVEREIGN

The three "omnies" also tell us God is *sovereign*. No higher authority exists, and no one can stop Him from doing what He intends. Psalm 115:3 says, "God is in the heavens; He does whatever He pleases." But, Psalm 115:16 also proclaims, "The heavens are the heavens of the Lord, but the earth He has given to the sons of men." These and other verses remind us that while the Almighty reigns as the highest possible authority, He also gives humanity a measure of freedom and authority as *stewards* of this planet. The Lord never stops being sovereign, but He does give us a limited ability to rule over the affairs of our planet.

Understanding the coexistence of God's sovereignty and human freedom helps us make sense of injustice and abuse. The Lord reigns over the earth, but He does not control all that happens. Even so, He can turn our trauma for good and will one day call abusers into account.

IMMUTABLE

God's *immutability* is another seemingly confusing term with a simple meaning: *the Lord does not change* (Malachi 3:6; James 1:17). Our Creator cannot become more or less of what He already is. How can anyone improve upon what is whole and perfect? Perhaps we can state it another way by saying God is never moody. You will get the same God every time you approach Him in prayer. I am so thankful I do not have to worry about someone so powerful ever saying, "Get out of My face! I've had a really bad day in the Andromeda Galaxy!"

ETERNAL

If you want to get your brain synapses firing, consider the *eternal* nature of God. How do we measure time? We follow the movements of celestial bodies such as sun, moon, and earth. How did those celestial bodies come into existence? God created them. That means

He created time and exists outside of it. You will never catch heaven's King wearing a watch! We read in the Bible that "with the Lord one day is like a thousand years, and a thousand years like one day" (2 Peter 3:8). Human and animal life remains subject to the clock; the Creator of that life does not.

HOLY

The book of Revelation records a scene in which four strange creatures worship before heaven's throne proclaiming, "Holy, holy, holy is the Lord God, the Almighty, who was and who is and who is to come" (Revelation 4:8). Of the many things they could say, the four creatures proclaim God's *holiness*. And while we can identify several nuances to the meaning of *holy*, the basic idea is that God is in a league of His own. No one is like Him, He alone is worthy of all worship and honor, and He is set apart from the commonality and corruption of our world. If we stopped here, I think I would be terrified, but thankfully, we can identify several other attributes that characterize our Creator.

GOOD

To understand the kingdom of God we must first learn about the King, for the kingdom is the domain of the King. And thankfully for us, the King is *good*. In Psalm 25:8, we read, "Good and upright is the Lord; therefore He instructs sinners in the way." Everything about God is good, and there is nothing bad to be found in Him. That means everything He does is also good. We might not always understand His actions, but we can always trust the Lord's goodness.

JUST

Having spent as much time in God's presence as anyone, and having seen judgment from heaven on many occasions, Moses proclaimed at the end of his life, "The Rock! His work is perfect, for all His ways are just; a God of faithfulness and without injustice, righteous and upright is He" (Deuteronomy 32:4). Moses had a front-row seat in God's theater, and He came away impressed by the Lord's commitment to *justice*.

MERCIFUL

The two might seem to contradict, but God is *merciful* as well as just. King David, who had experienced the discipline of God, praised Him by saying, "The Lord is gracious and merciful; slow to anger and great in lovingkindness" (Psalm 145:8). Through the cross of Jesus Christ, we see both justice and mercy on full display. Jesus took upon Himself the penalty for our sins so justice might be served against our transgressions. This He did as the highest expression of mercy toward a wayward people.

JOYFUL

Some people think of God as being wrathful. And while we dare not ignore His anger over sin and injustice, heaven does not revolve around what happens on earth. It is *joy* that characterizes the Lord of heaven. Again, from the Psalms we read, "In Your presence is fullness of joy; in Your right hand there are pleasures forever" (Psalm 16:11). And from the apostle Paul we learn that "the kingdom of God is not eating and drinking, but righteousness and peace and joy in the Holy Spirit" (Romans 14:17).

LOVING AND FAITHFUL

I find it difficult to separate God's *love* from His *faithfulness*. As King David worshiped, he penned, "Your lovingkindness, O Lord, extends to the heavens, Your faithfulness reaches to the skies" (Psalm 36:5). Faithful love—in our vast sea of emotional needs, nothing compares!

My wife's attitude toward our grandchildren reminds me of the Lord's faithful love. When she goes out shopping, Debi has those kids in mind. They have stolen her heart, and she is always looking for ways to bless. There is no sense of obligation on Debi's part—only goodwill that flows from deeply rooted love.

Our heavenly Father makes promises to His children because He cares deeply about us. And He will be ever faithful to the promises flowing from His heart of love. God's faithful love will never falter—no matter what we do or do not do.

Being abandoned ranks at the very bottom of our human experiences, and how easy it is to feel alone in this world with no one really caring! But God is an *advocate* for His children, faithfully watching over them and always seeking their best interests. The universe does not care, but our Creator does—deeply.

Those who are paranoid believe the world is conspiring against them. But another word, *pronoia*, portrays the opposite state of mind. For Christians, pronoia represents the realization of a "divine conspiracy" for our good. The shepherd David said it best: "Surely goodness and lovingkindness will follow [hound] me all the days of my life, and I will dwell in the house of the Lord forever" (Psalm 23:6).

When I look back over my life as a Christian, I cannot say I have always felt as though God was with me. And yes, there have been times of extreme difficulty. But when I survey the big picture, I am amazed by His favor and care through even the worst situations. Regardless of what other people do, I find comfort, peace, and security in His faithful love.

TRUTH BEGETS CONFIDENCE

Some people think it does not matter what we believe about God as long as we are sincere in our beliefs. But such a mentality proclaims that what we believe matters more than who God is. And when our personal beliefs matter more than God's reality, our world becomes unstable and insecure.

An existence defined by "your truth" or "my truth" is driven by human opinions. So while the idea of personal truths might resonate in a classroom or coffee shop, it does little to help us navigate the very real difficulties of life on our planet. Only as we lean into the reality of God can we find a source of security that the circumstances of this world will never shake.

Our Creator might not always look good from our limited perspective, and His actions might not always appear just, but He is *always worthy* of our trust. Those who trust in a nebulous, uncaring universe will find themselves alone and abandoned when they need help most. But those who rest their confidence in our good and faithful God can experience peace and security even in the midst of chaos.

Digging Deeper
Into Chapter Three

Who creates whom? Genesis 1:27 tells us God created humanity *in His image*. But that is not how this world thinks.

Dig deeper: Genesis 1:26-28

History and archaeology have revealed an abundance of "gods" that were created by human imaginations. And people can become indignant if we question whether those images are rooted in reality.

Today, when we speak of Roman mythology, few people believe the twelve primary gods and goddesses were actually real. But it was the very same Roman Empire that tortured and killed Christians for refusing to worship their array of supposed deities. This leads us to question who has the right to do the creating.

To answer this question, we begin by recognizing the nature of the spiritual realm. Unseen does not equal unreal. My eyes cannot see radio waves, but turning on my car stereo reminds me of their existence. Nor can I declare those radio waves to be what I want them to be. I might be free to choose the station (depending on whether my wife is in the passenger seat), but I cannot choose what songs the station plays.

The spiritual realm is either real or imaginary. We either seek to understand the spiritual, or to create it through our own musings. A key word is *truth*. Truth is reality, and reality is truth. We all have our own perceptions and opinions, but truth is *objective*. It does not depend upon our thoughts or perspectives.

Jesus said He came to testify of truth (John 18:37). What was He saying? To paraphrase, "I am here to reveal and declare the spiritual reality surrounding us. If you want to know what is true, if you care about truth more than your own opinions and desires, you will listen to what I say and teach."

Dig deeper: John 17:13-19
John 18:33-38

Through His many teachings, Jesus sought to bring people into alignment with the unseen spiritual reality surrounding us. As those created by the Almighty, it falls upon us to seek truth and align our lives accordingly. Only in our own minds do we have the right and power to recreate God in our image.

See also: John 4:7-26

Would you like to save yourself immeasurable frustration and grief? Acknowledge that you are an imperfect, created being who is subject to the self-existent, sovereign Creator of our seemingly infinite cosmos. Getting that reality settled in our hearts is the vital first step toward a truly meaningful existence.

Through the eyes of a broken world, accepting a submissive role might provoke images of hopeless captivity in a cruel, foreign land. But ours is a grand journey of discovery as we spend our lives embracing fresh dimensions of God's goodness.

I find it difficult to express how amazing is the opportunity before us to intimately know the Creator of all things. In His profound wisdom, God will even use down and difficult days to reveal His goodness to the humble-hearted. Never let anyone tell you otherwise; the King of Glory wants *you* to know Him personally.

Dig deeper: Jeremiah 29:11-13

QUESTIONS

1. Why is it foolish to put our trust in an impersonal universe?
2. Why do people seem to equate *spiritually unseen* with *unreal*?
3. What attribute of God moves your heart most?
4. Why must we see God as a seamless whole?
5. What does it mean to you that our Creator is good?
6. Why is it vital for us to align with the Lord's created order?

Chapter 4
Creation

"In the beginning God created the heavens and the earth" (Genesis 1:1). I could not think of a better way for the Bible to begin! Humans have always been a minuscule part of the universe. Despite our advanced technology, we cannot even begin to see all that is out there, let alone explain how it came into being. Peering back through the corridors of time, we catch only glimpses of the mysterious deep.

The beginning is a starting place created by the One who has no beginning or end. Everything begins and ends with God. He continues to work out a good, albeit mysterious, plan.

Another way of looking at our situation involves a *creation/fall/redemption* paradigm. Within the Bible, we find good news, bad news, and the best news imaginable. God created all things good. Humanity chose death by disobeying Him. Still, the Lord provided an ingenious plan to redeem sinful souls. However, some of us struggle to accept this reality, having run head-on into the supposed roadblock of science.

Some scientists confidently proclaim that creation burst into existence out of nothing and evolved to profound levels of complexity solely by natural means. But having a science background myself, I can say that such claims regarding our origins are built upon unstable foundations. Our attempts to explain our origins involve peering into the unknown far more than standing on absolute certainties.

SCIENCE VERSUS FAITH?

From a young age, scientific curiosity stirred my heart with a thirst for deeper knowledge. And it was while pursuing a chemistry degree that I picked up the mantle of theology. The two do not clash nearly as much as I was once led to believe. Theology focuses on the "whys" of our existence, and science the "hows." Practically every major field of science was established by a person of faith who was trying to understand God's creation better.

The principles of science and theology are similar—at least they should be—involving objective pursuits to understand reality (truth). The major difference is that science deals in the realm of our natural, physical existence and theology our supernatural, unseen world.

Those who elevate science and discount theology do a terrible disservice to humanity. Abandoning the moral foundation theology provides, they have helped foster a "survival of the fittest" world driven by selfish interests. It is for this reason I often say, "I don't have a problem with science; it's *scientists* that concern me."

As noble as the idea of objective scientific study might sound, it is a realm filled with pressure to conform—and to pursue positions, money, and fame. In recent years, we have seen an escalating number of retractions from scientific journals. This is largely because ethical scientists have pressured academic journals to deal with widespread error and fraud.[1] And with an increasingly fragile moral foundation—weakened by their own efforts—members of the scientific community face more and more temptation to succeed by any means possible.

I present these ideas not to argue for the scientific validity of the creation story in Genesis—I do not see it as a scientific document—but to caution the reader against discounting the Bible on supposedly scientific grounds. If we keep the primary goals of Scripture in mind, Genesis shines like a gleaming star on a clear night.

> All Scripture is inspired by God and profitable for teaching, for reproof, for correction, for training in righteousness; so that the man of God may be adequate, equipped for every good work.
> 2 Timothy 3:16–17

GEMS FROM GENESIS

In the book of Genesis, we discover sacred gems that open our eyes to our Creator's eternal purposes regarding humanity. Patterns and tendencies identified early in the book help explain both the dynamics of our existence and the wisdom of God's plan.

---

1. *Retraction Watch* (blog), accessed February 20, 2025, https://retractionwatch.com/.

The first two chapters of Genesis highlight the seven "days" of creation. The original language is not clear about whether they were literal days, but that is not the primary point. *Genesis begins the story of God's relationship with humanity, and that is what matters most.*

In the first chapter, we see a stark contrast between humanity and the rest of creation:

> Then God said, "Let Us make man in Our image, according to Our likeness; and let them rule over the fish of the sea and over the birds of the sky and over the cattle and over all the earth, and over every creeping thing that creeps on the earth." God created man in His own image, in the image of God He created him; male and female He created them. God blessed them; and God said to them, "Be fruitful and multiply, and fill the earth, and subdue it; and rule over the fish of the sea and over the birds of the sky and over every living thing that moves on the earth."
> Genesis 1:26–28

Made in God's very image, Adam and Eve stood as the *crown jewels* of His creative efforts. But how can we fathom the significance of being formed in the image of the King of Glory? The idea sets humanity apart—even from the angels.[2] Humans are unique in both complexity and design. No other created beings have been blessed like us with purpose, stewardship over the earth, moral bearings, and most important of all, the potential for an intimate relationship with the God who created us.

Having formed humanity uniquely in His image, the Lord provided an extra blessing by placing Adam and Eve in the *garden of Eden* (Genesis 2:8). The Hebrew word *Eden* carries the meaning of luxury and delight—like a fine delicacy that is delightful to eat.[3] From the beginning, God intended His human jewels to dwell in *paradise*. What a powerful realization!

If you won a vacation in "paradise" from a reputable company, what thoughts would run through your mind? Would you think about

---

2. As appealing as the idea might sound, humans do not become angels after they die.
3. Robert L. Thomas, *New American Standard Hebrew-Aramaic and Greek Dictionaries: Updated Edition* (Anaheim: Foundation Publications, Inc., 1998).

peace and ease? Pleasure and luxury? Beauty? Abundance? Freedom? All were markers of God's good design for humanity in Eden.

Not only were their needs met, but Adam and Eve were also given unlimited *freedom* to eat from any tree of the garden but one:

> Then the LORD God took the man and put him into the garden of Eden to cultivate it and keep it. The LORD God commanded the man, saying, "From any tree of the garden you may eat freely; but from the tree of the knowledge of good and evil you shall not eat, for in the day that you eat from it you will surely die." Genesis 2:15–17

Some people think Christianity is about following rules, but in Eden, we find only *one* protective restriction. This boundary was necessary because, being of the created order, humans can never know unrestricted freedom. We will always be subject to the need for God's provision, and His command provided that reminder.

DELIGHT

Paradise is not self-existent. It is made paradise by the Almighty's presence, and it carries the same sense of delight expressed by His wisdom in the creation of our world.

> When He set for the sea its boundary
> So that the water would not transgress His command,
> When He marked out the foundations of the earth;
> Then I was beside Him, as a master workman;
> And I was daily His delight,
> Rejoicing always before Him,
> Rejoicing in the world, His earth,
> And having my delight in the sons of men.
> Proverbs 8:29–31

Gazing upon humans—the pinnacle of His creative efforts—God not only saw goodness, but also took great pleasure. And though our circumstances have changed, His core feelings toward us have not.

Digging Deeper Into Chapter Four

The Genesee River begins its course in northern Pennsylvania as multiple branches join to form the main body. Crossing the New York border, the river flows north to Lake Ontario, widening as it goes. Scenic falls cascade in Letchworth State Park, but as the Genesee grows larger, the water becomes increasingly silty and opaque.

Skaneateles—a sixteen-mile-long Finger Lake in central New York—differs greatly. Skaneateles is purported to be one of the cleanest lakes in the United States. Several municipalities have even used it as an unfiltered source of drinking water. The lake is so clear that I found it impossible to estimate the depth while gazing at the rocks below.

The contrast between the Genesee River and Skaneateles Lake reminds me of the struggle between scientists and theologians to explain the origins of our existence. Both groups want to claim "Skaneateles clarity," while reality is closer to "Genesee murkiness."

We have no video record and cannot time travel to observe what transpired back then. Our scientific knowledge is also incomplete, sometimes changing as new discoveries come to light. And we are unable to perform experiments that would replicate early environments.

Scientists surprisingly discovered *soft tissue* in dinosaur fossils that were supposedly tens of millions of years old. Apparently, no one had bothered to look because no one thought it possible for fragile organic materials to survive so long. Further study has led to the idea that iron in the blood helped preserve the materials.[4] A laboratory experiment found that ostrich blood vessels soaked in an iron-rich solution made of red blood cells remained recognizable after a two-year period. The experiment seemed to satisfy many questioning minds.

---

4. Stephanie Pappas, *Controversial T. Rex Soft Tissue Find Finally Explained*, Live Science, November 26, 2013, accessed February 20, 2025, https://www.livescience.com/41537-t-rex-soft-tissue.html.

Consider the limitations of such a study. *Two years* in a lab does not provide even a faint reflection of *70 million years* in an uncontrolled environment. Scientists have no grounds to regard theories as facts, and yet many academics treat naturalistic evolution as a scientific fact. Honest inquirers must claim "Genesee River!" and not "Skaneateles Lake!" when trying to understand or explain the details of our origins.

Dig deeper: Genesis 1

The first two chapters of Genesis help clarify our vision to better see God apart from the corruption of sin and the blight of a broken world. We cannot entirely grasp the Lord's reasoning for every aspect of His design, but we can see His unfiltered goodness in the creation of Adam and Eve and the free, luxurious paradise He provided for them.

Dig deeper: Genesis 2

Naturally, we are inclined to question why a good God would allow the scourge of evil to enter our world, but the answer need not be complicated. For humanity to experience eternal bliss, we must know our place in God's divine order of the universe, and that could happen only by allowing us to eat the rotten fruit of prideful choices.[5]

We should also note that the Bible *begins* and *ends* with paradise, meaning luxury, joy, and life have always been at the heart of God's intentions for us. We just need to do things *His* way.

Dig deeper: Revelation 22

QUESTIONS

1. What is the importance of Genesis 1:1?
2. Why is the *creation/fall/redemption* paradigm significant?
3. How should science and theology complement one another?
4. What makes humanity unique?
5. What does it mean to be created in God's image?
6. What message does God's delight in creation communicate?

---

[5]. Of all my books, *The Age of Abiding: Experiencing the Life of the Vine* provides the most complete and concise explanation of these events.

Chapter 5
The Crash

"Well, that was a good meal!" I said with a satisfied smile as Debi and I walked out of a trendy restaurant with a friend. I was not making immediate comparisons, but a few bad meals with unpleasant companions undoubtedly influenced my perspective.

For humanity, *good* is a relative term, made meaningful by a lifetime of experiences. Action, suspense, and success will mark a "good" ball game. But witnessing boring games, in which a favorite team loses badly, makes the good so much more meaningful. Good is a matter of comparison—most often to expected standards.

When Jesus came proclaiming the "good news" of the kingdom, the people of His day felt acutely aware of the bad. They had tasted the heartbreak and frustration of living under oppressive Roman rule, and their nation was also being corrupted from within by greedy and power-hungry leaders.

HUMANITY'S BAD CHOICE

The idea of good news is mostly built upon the premise of bad news prior. And as much as we might want to avoid talking about negative issues, we cannot grasp the depth and breadth of the gospel apart from a basic understanding of our bad history. *Christ's good news is better than most people realize because humanity's bad is worse than many are willing to accept.*

Being created in God's image meant that Adam and Eve were given the freedom and capacity to love, which also meant He gave them the freedom and capacity to not love. And so it was that the Lord provided the crowns of His creation with a choice between life and death, introducing the concepts of good and evil in the process. From Genesis 3, we discover what happened next:

> Now the serpent was more crafty than any beast of the field which the LORD God had made. And he said to the woman, "Indeed, has God said, 'You shall not eat from any tree of the garden'?" The woman said to the serpent, "From the fruit of the trees of the garden we may eat; but from the fruit of the tree which is in the middle of the garden, God has said, 'You shall not eat from it or touch it, or you will die.'" The serpent said to the woman, "You surely will not die! For God knows that in the day you eat from it your eyes will be opened, and you will be like God, knowing good and evil." When the woman saw that the tree was good for food, and that it was a delight to the eyes, and that the tree was desirable to make one wise, she took from its fruit and ate; and she gave also to her husband with her, and he ate. Then the eyes of both of them were opened, and they knew that they were naked; and they sewed fig leaves together and made themselves loin coverings.
>
> They heard the sound of the LORD God walking in the garden in the cool of the day, and the man and his wife hid themselves from the presence of the LORD God among the trees of the garden. Genesis 3:1–8

Some see the Genesis story of Adam, Eve, and the two trees as mythological fantasy, but I see a profoundly insightful narrative on human nature and our current state. People do what they do for real reasons, and those reasons find their roots in early Genesis.

THE IRONIC, EVIL ROOT OF PRIDE

Why did Adam and Eve disobey their Creator and eat from the tree of the knowledge of good and evil? They wanted to be like God. But in an irony of all ironies, they had *already* been created in His image. Our first ancestors were as much like God as they were going to be. This means the temptation was not as much to be like God as it was to be like God *apart from* God. The alluring message promised a vibrant *independence* from the source of all life. But immediately after eating, humanity received its first bad news with crystal clarity.

The Crash

Adam and Eve disobeyed a stark warning from their Creator. In doing so, they joined a treasonous rebellion led by the fallen angel Lucifer—now disguised as a serpent—against God and His kingdom. And perhaps worst of all, their decision to trust the serpent over God has left a long trail of broken relationships, suffering, and death.

Many in our world would challenge my characterization of humanity's inherent sinfulness. Some see good people and bad people—like those who help others during times of crises and those who exploit. Others believe we all start with a clean slate and are influenced by the environments in which we grow up. And while there might be elements of truth to both perspectives, the Bible contends we are all inherently flawed (Romans 3:23; Galatians 3:22). Perhaps I could proclaim myself to be a good person compared to some other humans, but I could never make such a statement compared to a pure and holy God.

Humanity's terrible blight involves a broad thread of pride running through every person's heart. I am not referring to a sense of dignity that recognizes one's inherent worth, but a deep-rooted desire to compete with the status of God. This pervasive pride has four primary elements—all of which relate to Lucifer's failed attempt to overthrow the King of heaven (see Isaiah 14:12-14):

- **Self-centeredness** - One of the amazing things about God is that He is at the *center of the universe*, and yet is not self-centered. But that is not the case with those who want to be like God apart from God. Soon after being born into this world, we begin to expect everyone and everything to revolve around us. Only with consistent effort and persistent discipline can our parents teach us to be other-centered.

- **Self-sovereignty** - God is *sovereign*, meaning that He stands as the *highest authority* in existence. It seems foolish for us to seek such status, but the self-will influences human hearts like nothing else. Even more, we often lust for power, or at the very least, we seek to control the people and circumstances around us. Efforts toward control might be intentional or simply innate, but they compete against God and rob us of peace and joy regardless.

- **Self-glorification** - God is good within Himself, and all goodness flows from Him. Even more, our Creator is *glorious* in every way. Goodness and glory come *only* from the Author of creation, but we ever seek to find them within ourselves apart from Him. This pursuit is expressed through our individual and collective quests for a meaningful *identity*. A close examination will reveal that our never-ending pursuit of a positive self-image naturally finds its roots in common human pride. Sadly, this root of pride also hinders us from admitting we are flawed and in need of a Savior.

- **Self-sufficiency** - Our Creator has always been *self-existent*, needing nothing and no one to flourish. All things exist through Him, and He exists apart from all things. But there runs yet another root in our hearts that seeks to proclaim with pride, "I can be good by myself!"

Independence is what humanity wanted, and being separated from God is what humanity got. That is why Genesis 3 ends with the worst news possible:

> Then the LORD God said, "Behold, the man has become like one of Us, knowing good and evil; and now, he might stretch out his hand, and take also from the tree of life, and eat, and live forever"— therefore the LORD God sent him out from the garden of Eden, to cultivate the ground from which he was taken. So He drove the man out; and at the east of the garden of Eden He stationed the cherubim and the flaming sword which turned every direction to guard the way to the tree of life. Genesis 3:22–24

It might not seem fair that we would pay so steep a price for the sins of our ancestors, but that is the nature of reality. We are all interconnected, and our actions influence others even as we tell ourselves otherwise. Thankfully, God is good, and He birthed a good plan to restore the relationship humanity had severed. That is why we must always allow our Creator to write the end of the story.

Digging Deeper Into Chapter Five

There were not many "moving pieces" in the story of humanity's fall. God, two trees, two people, and a serpent. But, oh, what pain and confusion resulted from the misguided choice made by Adam and Eve!

We question why a wise and loving God would have planted the tree of the knowledge of good and evil in the garden, and even more, why He would have allowed the serpent access. One universal truth sums it up best: *God is so magnificent that the temptation to vie for His throne would always endanger any creature gazing upon His unrivaled glory.*

Allowing humanity access to the tree of the knowledge of good and evil was by no means an act of negligence, ignorance, or cruelty on God's part. It was part of a wise and loving plan to eliminate an ever-present threat so humans can inhabit paradise forever.

To better understand God's plan, we must travel back in time to a world outside our own. Two passages from the Old Testament provide us with *prophetic* accounts of what transpired when an archangel became enamored with glory. We call that angel "Lucifer," which is essentially the Latin rendering of *light bearer*.[1]

Two accounts found in Isaiah and Ezekiel are examples of what some call "near and far prophecy." The "near" elements refer to the earthly kings of Babylon and Tyre. And in both cases, the "far" speaks of the downfall of Lucifer—one of the greatest of all angels.

Dig deeper: Isaiah 14:3–21
Ezekiel 28:11–19

Intoxicated by God's glory, and enamored with his own beauty (which he was gifted as a created being), Lucifer began to lust for God's throne. Recruiting a third of the angels, he then made a violent play for that

---
[1]. James Swanson, *Dictionary of Biblical Languages with Semantic Domains: Hebrew (Old Testament)* (Oak Harbor, WA: Logos Research Systems, Inc., 1997).

seat of sovereign power. Blinded by pride, Lucifer could not have made a more foolish move because the Lord of creation has no peer.

Humiliated in defeat, Lucifer and his co-conspirators were thrown from heaven, and earth is where they landed. There has never been, and there will never be, a balance of power between God and anyone else. The King of heaven always reigns supreme.

Dig deeper: Revelation 12:7–9

The story sounds mythical, I know. But the Bible is clear about the wiles of the devil, and the existence of evil as a dark force in this world cannot be explained from a natural scientific perspective.

Dig deeper: Matthew 4:1–11

Filled with hatred, the devil ever seeks to steal, kill, and destroy. But in the end, even evil will serve the Almighty's purposes. The story of the cross illustrates this reality best. The devil sought to destroy Jesus, and wicked human hearts had Him crucified, but God turned it around for good by accomplishing the most powerful feat possible. We might not understand all the dynamics involved, but we can rest assured of heavenly triumph.

The devil is a pitiful creature, but never to be pitied. We should not be ignorant of his schemes, though those who have been forgiven of their sins and indwelt with the Holy Spirit have nothing to fear.

Dig deeper: 2 Corinthians 2:10–17

QUESTIONS

1. What makes the good news of the gospel so good?
2. How do you see self-centeredness at work in our world?
3. How do you see self-sovereignty at work in our world?
4. How do you see self-glorification at work in our world?
5. How do you see self-sufficiency at work in our world?
6. Why is independence from God the last thing we should ever seek?

Chapter 6
Laws of the Kingdom

If you take a few minutes to ponder heaven, what comes to mind? Gleaming streets of gold? Magnificent mansions? Revelation 22—the last chapter of the Bible—provides my favorite description:

> Then he showed me a river of the water of life, clear as crystal, coming from the throne of God and of the Lamb, in the middle of its street. On either side of the river was the tree of life, bearing twelve kinds of fruit, yielding its fruit every month; and the leaves of the tree were for the healing of the nations. There will no longer be any curse; and the throne of God and of the Lamb will be in it, and His bond-servants will serve Him; they will see His face, and His name will be on their foreheads. And there will no longer be any night; and they will not have need of the light of a lamp nor the light of the sun, because the Lord God will illumine them; and they will reign forever and ever. Revelation 22:1–5

This inspiring passage brings peace to my heart and fills me with hope for the future. Contrast the scene with some of the crime-infested, poverty-stricken areas of our world, and the apostle John's description of heaven becomes all the more meaningful.

KINGDOM STANDARDS

The kingdom of God is essentially the kingdom of heaven expressed on earthly soil. So how do we make the taste of paradise found in Revelation 22 our personal reality? We *align* our lives with His eternal kingdom by embracing its mindsets, laws, and dynamics.

Every government has its own sets of laws that even noncitizens are required to obey. And a person need violate only one statute to be considered a lawbreaker.

A while back, government authorities in the Turks and Caicos Islands detained several U.S. citizens for carrying ammunition in their luggage. They were not participating in a coup attempt. Nor were they planning anything malicious. These vacationers simply broke the law of the land and were thus deemed "lawbreakers." It did not matter that they had no guns, or that the ammo was mistakenly left from past hunting trips. Twelve years in prison for a forgotten cartridge might seem extreme, but that was the law of the land at the time. Thankfully for those detained, pressure from the U.S. government and the fear of losing tourist dollars limited their jail time and the dollar amount of fines they were required to pay.

As unfair or unreasonable government laws are at times, lawlessness can be worse still. When people do whatever they want, injustice and oppression will prevail. And if you add corruption into the mix, life can become miserable for a nation's citizens.

The kingdom of God provides the highest ideal for a government. But it is also a *sovereign* state with its own system of laws. The laws are the rule of the land, and no one has the power or authority to challenge them. Citizenship in the kingdom is voluntary; our Creator does not force us to follow His ways. But if we want the mind-stretching benefits of God's good reign, we must conform to His design.

When it comes to meeting the standards of heaven's paradise, we have only two options. The first involves self-effort and the second God's provision. As we explore these options, we soon realize only one path is viable. Let us begin with some challenging words spoken by Jesus during His Sermon on the Mount:

> When Jesus saw the crowds, He went up on the mountain; and after He sat down, His disciples came to Him. He opened His mouth and began to teach them, saying,
>
> "Blessed are the poor in spirit, for theirs is the kingdom of heaven.
> "Blessed are those who mourn, for they shall be comforted.
> "Blessed are the gentle, for they shall inherit the earth.

> "Blessed are those who hunger and thirst for righteousness, for they shall be satisfied.
> "Blessed are the merciful, for they shall receive mercy.
> "Blessed are the pure in heart, for they shall see God.
> "Blessed are the peacemakers, for they shall be called sons of God.
> "Blessed are those who have been persecuted for the sake of righteousness, for theirs is the kingdom of heaven."
> Matthew 5:1–10

Very early in His ministry, Jesus confronted the religious thinking of the day. The Jewish people, led by the Pharisees, Sadducees, and scribes, had become preoccupied with following religious rituals. They lost sight of what matters most: the state of our hearts and how we relate to one another. Blinded by self-righteous pride, the religious leaders felt they stood head and shoulders above the rest, when in reality, their self-centered ways had been distancing them from the Lord.

> "For I say to you that unless your righteousness surpasses that of the scribes and Pharisees, you will not enter the kingdom of heaven." Matthew 5:20

Through His Sermon on the Mount, Jesus called the Jewish people back to God's paradigm, but He did not stop there. The Son of God began to outline moral standards so high that even the most pious would have begun to squirm. Just calling another person a fool makes one guilty of a fiery hell (Matthew 5:22). And looking at a woman with lust equates to committing adultery (Matthew 5:28). Jesus added several other lofty standards, but I think you get the idea. In that self-righteous religious environment, the Son of God began His ministry with a compelling idea: *those who want to find acceptance with God through self-effort must meet heaven's standards of perfection.*

HOW GOOD ARE YOU?

I cannot stress enough the importance of this issue. So many times, I have heard statements such as, "Of course God will welcome me through the gates of heaven because I am basically a good person. I treat others decently, don't steal, don't lie—at least not very much—and even help those in need. Certainly, heaven will welcome people such as me."

But consider the Ten Commandments (Exodus 20:1-17). Have you ever spoken the Lord's name in vain? Dishonored your mother or father in any way? Stolen? Lied? Coveted what someone else had? I am not a gambler, but I would be willing to bet you have broken more than one of the commandments.

Now, let us consider a New Testament standard found in the Gospel of Matthew:

> One of them, a lawyer, asked Him a question, testing Him, "Teacher, which is the great commandment in the Law?" And He said to him, "'You shall love the Lord your God with all your heart, and with all your soul, and with all your mind.' This is the great and foremost commandment. The second is like it, 'You shall love your neighbor as yourself.' On these two commandments depend the whole Law and the Prophets." Matthew 22:35-40

Can you measure up to even one of the two primary laws that characterize God's kingdom? Do you love the Lord with *all* your heart, soul, and mind, *always* putting His desires before your own? And do you love your neighbors as yourself, *always* considering their needs to be as important as yours? The Ten Commandments were really about love, and any failure to obey them reveals selfish pride in our hearts. Contempt, envy, and bitterness, which are all common to humanity, are also affronts to love. How can any of us call ourselves good when we fall so far short of heaven's standards?

God gave the Ten Commandments not to make us righteous, but to reveal our unrighteousness. I am beyond thankful that the story does not end with the old covenant, because there would be no good news otherwise. But, knowing how far we fall short of heaven's perfection, the Lord has lovingly provided a path to citizenship in His kingdom. In our next chapter, we will seek to understand how the glad tidings of the gospel are even better than we imagine.

Digging Deeper Into Chapter Six

Compelled by a desire to be like God apart from God, Adam and Eve ate from the tree of the knowledge of good and evil. Accustomed only to the pristine paradise God had created, they failed to realize the impossibility of such a feat. Not only is our Creator all-wise and all-powerful, He is also perfect in every way. Who can even begin to meet such a standard?

Heaven is also a perfect kingdom, functioning in perfect harmony. If you or I were to enter those pearly gates without being cleansed of sin's contamination, we would ruin it.

Not long ago, a kindly teacher died because she was trying to show compassion to a rabid bat that had somehow made its way into her classroom.[1] According to a friend, the woman tried to scoop up the bat to release it outside without harm. She was bitten in the process but failed to seek medical attention. By the time symptoms began to appear in a month's time, it was too late. If not treated early on, rabies is almost always 100% fatal.

Because rabies is both contagious and deadly, anyone who had contact with the woman, including household members and medical workers, required post-exposure vaccine shots. Compassion is not enough; dangerous diseases must be managed wisely. Otherwise, they will spread and destroy a multitude of lives in the process.

We can say something similar about self-righteous pride. The "disease" is always fatal, and if not properly quarantined, heaven would become a cauldron of death similar to what we see on earth.

Anyone who seeks to know God—in this or the next life—must accept a fundamental truth: none of us are pure enough to be allowed entry

---

1. A. Pawlowski, *"Teacher Bitten by Bat in Classroom Dies of Rabies,"* TODAY, November 29, 2024, accessed February 14, 2025, https://www.today.com/health/news/teacher-dies-rabies-bat-bite-rcna182215.

to His presence. Furthermore, nothing we do can ever make us pure enough. The deadly root of pride has taken root in all our hearts, and unless thoroughly eradicated, will corrupt any environment in which humans dwell.

See also: Romans 3:9–20

This might all sound like morbid news, and yet it is anything but. *If the Bible emphasizes our sinfulness, it is only to guide us toward the greater sufficiency of Christ.*

Dig deeper: Galatians 3:10–29

A primary key to grasping these concepts involves recognizing the role of law—and specifically the Mosaic law—in revealing the reality of one's spiritual state. *When the apostle Paul speaks negatively of the law, he is addressing our human compulsion to seek righteousness by law, to validate ourselves by measuring up to moral and religious standards.* Keeping this in mind as you read Paul's letters—especially Romans and Galatians—will help unlock your understanding of the Christian faith.

The law has never been our primary problem. Human nature's *response* to the law provides the corrupt ground in which sin breeds. Only as we establish this truth firmly in our hearts can we position ourselves to grasp the breadth and depth of the good news of Jesus Christ.

See also: Romans 3:21–28

QUESTIONS

1. As you read Revelation 22:1–5, what moves you most?
2. Why is it a lie to think that "good" people go to heaven?
3. How many of the Ten Commandments have you broken?
4. What makes pride deadly?
5. When the apostle Paul refers to law in a negative sense, what is his intention?
6. According to Galatians 3:23–24, what is the primary purpose of the Mosaic law?

Chapter 7

Taking the Path of Grace

I grew up in a small town abounding in both churches and bars. That mix also reflected the community as a whole. No small number of people attended church, and even church schools, but few seemed to represent the type of lifestyle I would expect from a follower of Jesus. Among my peers, most who had attended religious schools lived no differently than the rest—except perhaps that their behavior was a bit worse.

Many of the faithful church attenders in our community took God's name in vain, used bad language, lied at their convenience, drank to excess, caroused sexually, and treated others cruelly. Some of the more devout seemed to be genuinely good people, but surprisingly few represented what I would call a Biblical lifestyle. And the handful who tried were often mistreated by others.

I was no better—and I knew it—but neither was I any worse than the mainstream churchgoers. So I reasoned, "Why add the burden of church attendance and religious obligation to an already hard life?" Only after being exposed to a different kind of devotion did I begin to grasp the true nature of Christianity.

NEVER GOOD ENOUGH

Attending church would have added more weight to my already burdened heart. I innately understood aspects of my life needed to change and knew deep down I could not live up to the Bible's moral standards. You see, that is the problem with trying to appease God through our works; we can never measure up to heaven's perfection. How good do you have to be? How good can you be? The need for perfection weighs on our shoulders like rocks in a backpack.

Have you ever failed at something so miserably that you gave up trying? Many people begin a new year with good and noble intentions. Perhaps the goal is to lose weight by exercising and eating better. The first week or two goes well, but then life happens. A sickness, a crisis at work, or even a bad night's sleep can all throw our well-intentioned plans off-kilter. Then, from deep within a freezer, ice cream starts calling. And as our mood swings lower, its voice cries louder. In the blink of an eye, the weight loss plans have fallen by the wayside. And all too often, after failing times without number, we give up trying.

Such struggles are common—especially in the moral arenas of life. Discovering we cannot live perfectly, we reason it is better to have fun than be miserable. Our sinful lifestyles might not satisfy or fulfill us, but loose living feels better than wallowing in guilt and misery by trying to walk an impossibly narrow line.

THE PATH OF PRIDE

Not everyone embraces a path of abandon, of course. Many piously fulfill their religious duties, assuming God is pleased as long as they attend the required services and perform rituals properly. But how quickly self-righteous pride takes root! Soon "the devout" are lauding their own goodness, looking down with judgment upon those who fail to meet their cultivated standards. Judgmental attitudes and social stratification then create conflict and division of all kinds. This approach to life begins when we are young, but it is destructive on multiple levels.

From the earliest age, we are told, "Do this! Don't do that!" Well-meaning adults condition us to believe that doing good things makes us good, and doing bad things makes us bad. We beam with pride when our good actions are celebrated and stew in frustration when we cannot seem to measure up. And from the perspective of parents and other adults, life is so much better when kids follow the rules.

Perhaps you are one of the few with an admirable moral history. You rarely disobeyed your parents, never ran with the bad crowd, and always set a stellar example at school and work. But are you *perfect*? Can you say with all sincerity that your heart is morally flawless? If so, I would be inclined to think you are either deluded or lying.

Even if you think you are a pretty good person, to whom are you comparing yourself? The comparison game is tricky. If we compare ourselves to those who are worse, we begin to feel superior. But when someone more noble or righteous comes along, their good example casts us in a negative light. Regardless, we must all deal with the innate pride that contaminates the waters of our lives.

The U.S. government has determined that the maximum amount of mercury in drinking water should be no more than 2 ppb. That is two *parts per billion*. Some chemicals are even more toxic. A glass of water might be 99.9% pure, but that remaining 0.1% could be enough to kill. Our human bodies are similar. If I were 99.9% healthy and infected by only one small deadly virus, would you share a drink with me?

Almost all of us can find good elements in our lives, and that is where we want to rivet our focus. But the poison of death still runs through our veins. We know this because we all eventually expire. Death is the stark reality that shatters our illusions of control and the supposed supremacy of human thinking. The reality of death proclaims that our idea of good will always be subject to a Higher Authority. And to think that God will accept me because I am basically a good person remains an oversung myth.

THE PATH OF GRACE

It is here that the good news of the gospel emerges like the dawn of a pristine morning. *God's plan for salvation runs contrary to our typical thinking about being good, meeting moral standards, and observing religious rituals.* The gospel is not rocket science, but it is unnatural. God's path to glory does not require a PhD to understand, but it differs from our natural thought processes so much that we struggle to comprehend the profound beauty. That is why deeply affected people are inclined to write inspiring songs such as "Amazing Grace" to express their sense of wonder over a heavenly favor we cannot earn.

We are all flawed—deeply flawed—because of our innate pride with its Edenic roots. It all began with a choice to live independently of our Creator. So if we want to experience the blessings of God's kingdom, we must choose a path that depends more on Him than us. We call that way the "gospel of grace."

> And you were dead in your trespasses and sins, in which you formerly walked according to the course of this world, according to the prince of the power of the air, of the spirit that is now working in the sons of disobedience. Among them we too all formerly lived in the lusts of our flesh, indulging the desires of the flesh and of the mind, and were by nature children of wrath, even as the rest. But God, being rich in mercy, because of His great love with which He loved us, even when we were dead in our transgressions, made us alive together with Christ (by grace you have been saved), and raised us up with Him, and seated us with Him in the heavenly places in Christ Jesus, so that in the ages to come He might show the surpassing riches of His grace in kindness toward us in Christ Jesus. For by grace you have been saved through faith; and that not of yourselves, it is the gift of God; not as a result of works, so that no one may boast.
> Ephesians 2:1–9

Salvation by grace through faith. This is the path provided by God that leads to everlasting life. It lifts the burden of perfection from our shoulders and drives a stake through the heart of pride. Other systems of religious belief might provide a hint of grace, but only Biblical Christianity is *characterized* by grace. Only the good news of the gospel can free us from humanity's exhausting quest to always measure up.

We feel the compulsion to tightly grasp our sense of goodness, feeling that in some ways it is all we have. But this quest for self-righteousness becomes a stumbling block that hinders us from drawing near to God and experiencing His healing touch. Only as we let go do we discover a glorious, unshakeable identity as His beloved child.

Our Creator is omniscient. He knows everything that can possibly be known, including the deepest thoughts of our hearts. I am not suggesting we embrace a morbid "I'm a miserable creature" mindset, but that we admit our need and embrace the saving grace of the cross. God's plan for salvation is the remedy for our natural inclinations toward selfish pride. And so it is that the mysterious wisdom of grace separates the Christian faith from every other belief system. The path might seem unnatural, but it is the only one that truly transforms.

Digging Deeper Into Chapter Seven

How would you define *religion*? According to Webster's dictionary, it is "a personal set or institutionalized system of religious attitudes, beliefs, or practices."[1] Christianity certainly falls under this umbrella, but it also differs from other religions in a unique way.

Because Adam and Eve ate from the tree of the knowledge of good and evil, all humanity seeks to live up to standards in pursuit of personal validation and significance. We do this in virtually all arenas of life, including appearance, performance, knowledge, and possessions. This mindset of measuring up to self-validate also characterizes our religious mindset—regardless of the belief system involved.

Religious requirements might involve following rituals, offering sacrifices, praying at certain times of day, or donating money. And in most situations, there are laws and codes to ensure we do things the "right" way. Many religions also enfold moral elements, which can help order society and protect the vulnerable.

Regardless of the faith tradition, the bottom line is that we strive to measure up to standards in an effort to appease the divine. But the result of our efforts will be either pride or despair. Some will become self-righteous and judgmental because they believe they meet divine standards—especially compared to the unsavory among us. Others develop mindsets rooted in guilt and shame as their inability to measure up becomes painfully clear. And so it is that we divide humanity between the good and the bad, between those who meet our moral and religious standards, and those who do not.

Do we realize the ramifications? At the root of our quest to measure up lies the age-old desire to be like God apart from God. *But those seeking to live up to religious standards fail even when they succeed.*

---

1. *Merriam-Webster,* s.v. "religion," accessed February 14, 2025, https://www.merriam-webster.com/dictionary/religion.

How can this be? How can we do so well and so badly at the same time? The concept might seem complicated but the answer is simple: we are operating according to a human paradigm of self-effort rather than a divine one of grace.

If we want to comprehend the good news of the kingdom, we need a revelation of grace. The beauty—and power—of grace lies in it being *unearned. God's grace pulls away the podium on which pride stands.*

> See also: 1 Corinthians 1:18–31

By eating from the tree of the knowledge of good and evil, humanity chose to put itself under a paradigm of law. Through the Mosaic law, God used a system of civil, ceremonial, and moral standards to show all people are guilty of sin. But through the cross of Jesus Christ, the Lord created a pathway of grace by which we can find forgiveness of our sins and be freed from the exhausting burden of seeking to be righteous by measuring up to law-based standards.

> See also: Romans 5:1–11

Grace proclaims a powerful message of hope. No matter your family or religious background, or your moral history, the path of grace provides an opportunity for you to draw near to heaven's eternal King.

> See also: Romans 7:14–8:4

QUESTIONS

1. Have you ever been tempted to give up in an area of life because of repeated failure?
2. How does living by law-based standards for righteousness provide a platform for pride?
3. What makes pride deadly?
4. What makes the gospel unnatural?
5. What makes the gospel of grace a message of hope?
6. What burdens does the gospel remove from our shoulders?

Chapter 8

Wise Compassion

I cannot imagine God ever being confused. Or uncertain. Or at a loss about what to do next. And so I write in human terms to say He had a "dilemma" with humanity. The Lord loves people and wants them to be near, but we are naturally prideful and bent on our own way. Like a deadly virus or toxic agent, this pride swings open wide a door for death and destruction. How could He even begin to fix the problem?

Thankfully for us, our Creator is omniscient. He knows everything there is to know. There is no event He does not foresee or problem He cannot solve. Forget about you or the angels or anyone trying to befuddle the Lord with a question or problem. It will not happen.

GOD'S GOOD PLAN

As Adam and Eve sank their teeth into the forbidden fruit, heaven's King did not jolt to attention as if a surprise earthquake had struck. From before the beginning of time, God knew they would disobey His command. With wisdom and knowledge well beyond our grasp, the Creator of our cosmos set forth a good plan to produce an eternal paradise—one marked by love freely given. And though that plan includes a season of sometimes intense suffering on earth, Jesus chose to step down from the glory of heaven to enter our pain and humiliation.

I admit, it took me a long time to see the big picture. When I first started exploring God's plan in the Bible, it seemed nonsensical. But the more I prayed for wisdom, the more I realized the problem was with me. I now see our Creator's plan for redemption as nothing short of genius. Not only does it identify the key issues influencing our behavior, it also provides transformational remedies for those issues.

COMPASSION WITHOUT WISDOM

To think the Lord would grant us entrance to heaven because of His unconditional love is to commit the same error that has befallen many well-intentioned people. Exercising compassion without wisdom will create social chaos by welcoming lawlessness and creating cold, hard hearts in the process.

God's kingdom operates by a paradigm of love freely chosen. Its citizens regard one another with honor, respect, and esteem, choosing to put the interests of others above their own. But when people do not love one another, as is often the case in this world, government leaders must pass laws to discourage bad behavior and punish wrong actions. Otherwise, chaos will rule and the most vulnerable suffer.

A relevant example involves shame. In recent decades, psychologists have begun to recognize the toxic influence of shame in fostering bad behavior. The need for a meaningful identity has always stood at the core of our human existence, and when people lack such significance, they are inclined to abuse and mistreat others (and sometimes themselves). Consider mass shootings. The vast majority of those vile deeds are committed by young, insecure males who are trying to prove their manhood or make a name for themselves.

Children forge healthy identities primarily through family relationships, and through loving fathers in particular. I am not slighting mothers; they play their own vital roles in raising children to maturity. But if you examine the blight of violence plaguing America through an objective lens, you will find the lack of a healthy fatherly influence to be a key contributing factor.

Many academics recognize the vital role that nuclear families—and especially fathers—play in rearing emotionally healthy children to adulthood, but they cannot bring themselves to accept such a reality. Promoting the traditional family model runs against our desires for "free" sex, the acceptability of "alternative lifestyles," and a quest to eliminate what is often referred to as the "oppressive patriarchy."

Addressing root issues related to fatherlessness will not garner many research dollars or provide ready opportunities to publish in academic journals. So instead, we focus on topics such as patriarchy, social systems, and shame. But all too often, these efforts deny the innately corrupt nature of the human heart. Compassionate zeal then creates even worse problems.

In the eyes of a civilized society, it is shameful to be imprisoned for bad behavior. And so cultural wisdom reasons that if we remove sources of shame—such as incarceration—people will naturally reform themselves. But human nature does not function this way! Selfish and entitled hearts will always look for ways to "game" the system. Crime then escalates as laws go unenforced or consequences are minimized. Violence increases and innocent people unnecessarily become victims. Society then becomes more hardened and cynical—not more loving—as the consequences for illegal actions are minimized or eliminated. In contrast, God's good plan provides the means for hearts to be *transformed* so people no longer want to mistreat others.

Another relevant example relates to the heartbreaking problem of migrants and refugees in our oppressive, conflict-ridden world. Many nations are in a bad way because of war, crime, and famine. And as the pain of suffering increases, people understandably look for greener pastures. We should indeed care about those in such straits, but open-border policies have proven disastrous for nations that have welcomed all without a reasonable vetting process.

When we throw open the door to criminals, foreign spies, terrorists, and people who do not respect the laws of the land, we welcome lawlessness and chaos. Again, the innocent suffer, and again, people become more hardened and cynical in response to the chaos.

COMPASSION WITH WISDOM

You might think this chapter reads like a political commentary, but that is not my intent. I hope never to make the mistake of equating the platform of a political party with the essence of God's eternal kingdom. The Bible has long used physical illustrations to help explain spiritual truths, so I share these examples because of their relevance to our discussion. Heaven is destined to be an eternal paradise, but it cannot remain so unless access is limited and hearts transformed. The only other option would be to restrict free will, which society sees as perhaps the worst transgression of all.

God's plan is both wise and compassionate. We can identify it as *inclusive* in the sense that the Lord welcomes *all* to become citizens of His kingdom. Gender, race, nationality, and even moral history remain irrelevant to those seeking to become "naturalized" citizens. But God's kingdom will never welcome lawlessness. His government operates by laws of faith and love, and those unwilling to embrace His terms *exclude themselves* from kingdom citizenship.

GRACE

In the design of God's government, His grace looms large.

> For by grace you have been saved through faith; and that not of yourselves, it is the gift of God; not as a result of works, so that no one may boast. Ephesians 2:8–9

Mysterious almost beyond belief, grace provides a path to God that allows no opportunity for self-credit. Through grace, the King of Glory favors us in ways we cannot earn and do not deserve. In medical terms, we would identify grace as the only effective *antidote* to the deadly virus of selfish pride.

The influence of grace goes even beyond the idea of unearned favor. Through grace, God writes His laws upon our hearts so we desire to do His will. And through grace, He gives us power beyond our own ability to fulfill those purposes.

God's grace abounds like water in the ocean, but it is never a cheap commodity. Grace comes to us at a steep price through the cross of Jesus Christ, and that is what we must look to if we seek to grasp the good news of His kingdom. There is no redemption apart from the cross, but through Christ's sacrificial death we can experience blessings beyond measure—ones that our Creator has destined for us from before the foundation of the world.

Do we want paradise or chaos? Chaos comes easily as we follow our natural human thinking. But those seeking to experience paradise must tread God's wise path of grace through the cross of Jesus Christ.

Digging Deeper
Into Chapter Eight

Repent is not a word commonly used apart from religious settings. I never had a teacher start the beginning of the school year by calling us to repent from our summer escapades. Or a coach admonishing us to repent for watching too much TV or playing too many video games. And because *grace* and *repentance* are mostly foreign to our cultural mindsets, misunderstandings abound.

Repentance is integral to Biblical Christianity, and it involves both a *turning* and a *rethinking*. When we repent, we *renew* our mindsets and *change* our actions.

>   See also: Matthew 4:12-17
>   Romans 12:1-2

Participation in God's kingdom requires repentance on our part. But a faulty understanding of grace causes us to view repentance as unnecessary. Until we grasp accurately the relationship between the two, we will struggle to live out the Christian faith.

To begin, we remember that humanity naturally lives by law in pursuit of righteousness. By default, we try to measure up to standards so we can be accepted and approved. The kingdom of God, however, operates by grace. The gospel of grace calls us to abandon our self-efforts and embrace what Jesus has accomplished on our behalf. So when we repent, we embrace a new and radical way of thinking and living.

While others expend their life energies climbing, comparing, and judging, God calls His children to *rest* in the sufficiency of the cross. As we rest, we quit trying to measure up. And we also begin to release others from the same expectations. Such a lifestyle is unnatural, requiring first a choice and then a change of thinking. But as we receive a revelation of grace from the Holy Spirit and reinforce the message of grace through the Scriptures, our thinking begins to change.

The power of grace profoundly influences our hearts. As we abide (live) in God's grace, the Holy Spirit begins to cultivate sweet *spiritual fruit* within us. We play a vital role in the process, not by trying to measure up to standards, but by trusting in the cross, yielding to God's will, and saying no to fleshly desires.

Dig deeper: Romans 6:1–14

If we fail to live according to God's plan, we can resolve the issue by humbling ourselves, confessing our failure, and leaning into the cross of Christ. The process can be messy and tumultuous at times, but the long-term effect is nothing short of transformational. Grace is both simple and mysterious.

Grace does not provide a license to do as we want, but the power to live according to God's good plan. *Through grace, heaven's King accepts us as we are, but it is also through grace that He transforms the fabric of our lives.*

Dig deeper: Galatians 5:13–26

While our world tries to mimic the acceptance that comes through grace, it remains bankrupt of the power to transform human hearts. Worldly authorities might demand that people change their behavior, but they can never transform or empower people to live in victory over the power of sin.

Grace truly is amazing. May we turn from ungodly actions and renew our thinking to a mindset of heavenly grace!

QUESTIONS

1. What is the danger of exercising compassion without wisdom?
2. In what way is the kingdom of God inclusive?
3. In what way is the kingdom of God exclusive?
4. What does it mean to repent?
5. Why is repentance essential for kingdom living?
6. What makes grace amazing?

Chapter 9
Setting the Record Straight

Fortune cookies come from China. Napoleon Bonaparte was short. The word *Xmas* was crafted in a secular attempt to remove Christ from Christmas. Julius Caesar was born via caesarean section (and ate Caesar dressing). Viking warriors had horns protruding from their helmets. Wolves howl at a full moon. Mice prefer cheese. Lightning never strikes the same place twice. Touching a toad will give you warts. These are just a few of the many misconceptions people believe.

Not surprisingly, misconceptions also abound regarding Jesus Christ, who came to us as God in human flesh and the Savior of humanity. Thinking that Vikings wore horns means little apart from how a dedicated Minnesota fan might dress for an NFL football game, but misconceptions about Jesus can prove deadly. So let us look to the Bible to address several common misconceptions about Christ.

JESUS' EXISTENCE

One of the more bizarre claims states that the person who spurred the separation of the most widely used calendar into BC and AD never existed. Besides the extensive writings of early church fathers, multiple *non-Christian* sources confirm the existence of Jesus and many of the people, locations, and events recorded in the Bible. Specifically, the writings of Josephus, Tacitus, Pliny the Younger, and even an excerpt from the Jewish Talmud mention Jesus and/or His crucifixion.[1]

JESUS' NAME

The name *Jesus* is the English rendition (via Latin) of the Greek *Iesous*—a transliteration of the Hebrew name *Yeshua*. Different alphabets have

---
1. If you still have doubts, consider reading *The Historical Jesus: Ancient Evidence for the Life of Christ* by Dr. Gary R. Habermas.

led to different pronunciations, but all refer to the original name *Yehoshua* (transliterated in English as *Joshua*), meaning "God is salvation." *Christ* is more of a *title* than a name, coming from the Greek version of the Hebrew *Messiah*, which means the "anointed one."

THE OLD VERSUS THE NEW

Many people, including some devoted Christians, believe the "God of the Old Testament" (God the Father) differs from the "God of the New Testament" (Jesus). Jesus' own words should help put any confusion to rest: "He who has seen Me has seen the Father" (John 14:9). The writer of Hebrews also stated it beautifully: "And He [Jesus] is the radiance of His glory and the exact representation of His nature" (Hebrews 1:3a).

So why the confusion? The God of the Old Testament seems harsh and vindictive, while we tend to view Jesus through a lens of kindness and acceptance. Some critics will even point to stories of judgment in the Old Testament as cause for rejecting God entirely. How do we reconcile these differences?

The Old and New Testaments represent two very different *covenants*. The "old covenant" (i.e., Mosaic law) involved an extensive system of over *six hundred* rules and rituals. God gave the Mosaic law *in response* to humanity's decision to disobey Him and eat from the tree of the knowledge of good and evil. Law-based standards of good and evil require perfection, and those who fall short will experience judgments of varying severity. But the Mosaic law was intended as a *stepping stone* to a superior way of life.

Drawing from Galatians 3:19–29, we recognize the primary purpose of Moses' law was to *point us toward Christ*. As we recoil at the harsh judgments recorded in the Old Testament, we naturally think there should be a better way. That way is the person of Jesus Christ and the new covenant of grace He initiated through His own spilled blood.

JUDGMENT

Reading through the Old Testament, we will find many expressions of God's mercy. Similarly, in the New Testament, we find situations in which Jesus brought down the hammer of judgment on hardened hearts. To think that the Son of God judged no one is another error of epic proportions.

As He set His face toward the cross, Jesus violently overturned the tables of the money changers, who were charging exorbitant rates for sacrificial animals (Matthew 21:12–13). Later, in Matthew 23, we find humanity's Savior declaring eight "woes" upon the Pharisees for their uncaring, unjust, and hypocritical behavior.

The Lord then prophesied about the extreme judgment that would soon be unleashed upon the nation of Israel for their many sins, rejection of God's rule, and unjust treatment of Himself. You will not find it in the Bible, but the historical record of the destruction of Jerusalem in AD 70 is enough to make a person sick to the stomach.

Christ's proclamation from the Gospel of John summarizes these ideas far better than I ever could:

> "For God so loved the world, that He gave His only begotten Son, that whoever believes in Him shall not perish, but have eternal life. For God did not send the Son into the world to judge the world, but that the world might be saved through Him. He who believes in Him is not judged; he who does not believe has been judged already, because he has not believed in the name of the only begotten Son of God. This is the judgment, that the Light has come into the world, and men loved the darkness rather than the Light, for their deeds were evil." John 3:16–19

Through these words, Jesus has tossed the "judgment ball" back into our court. We choose to believe and move into the light of His love and truth—receiving eternal life and avoiding the pain of judgment—or we pursue our own way and eat the rotten fruit produced by sin.

JESUS' LIFESTYLE

If talk of judgment leaves you unsettled, please consider the following from Hebrews 4:

> Therefore, since we have a great high priest who has passed through the heavens, Jesus the Son of God, let us hold fast

our confession. For we do not have a high priest who cannot sympathize with our weaknesses, but One who has been tempted in all things as we are, yet without sin. Therefore let us draw near with confidence to the throne of grace, so that we may receive mercy and find grace to help in time of need. Hebrews 4:14–16

Jesus never sinned, and yet He intimately understands our pain and struggles. Living as the Son of Man, He faced the same kinds of temptations we all encounter. And while hanging on the cross as a sacrifice for our sins, He experienced the pain and despair that His sinless lifestyle would never invite. The Lord truly understands us and has opened wide the door for us to approach His throne of grace.

GOD WITH US

Some contend Jesus would be appalled by the idea of people falling at His feet to worship. This is another deadly error. Unlike the religious leaders of His day, Jesus modeled humility. Still, He was not shy about His true identity as God in human flesh. Nor were His followers.

Before going to the cross, Jesus proclaimed, "I am the way, and the truth, and the life; no one comes to the Father but through Me" (John 14:6b). Peter also affirmed His exclusive identity as Savior by saying, "There is salvation in no one else; for there is no other name under heaven that has been given among men by which we must be saved" (Acts 4:12). These statements cut like a knife but sparkle with clarity.

One of the more profound stories tells of the disciple Thomas' doubts about Christ's resurrection (John 20:24–29). Gracious, yet firm, the Lord challenged Thomas' unbelief by showing His scars. How did the disciple respond? "My Lord and my God!" If Jesus did not think Himself to be God, according to Jewish custom and law, He would have torn His clothes, appalled by the idea of false worship. Instead, the Lord responded by saying, "Because you have seen Me, have you believed? Blessed are they who did not see, and yet believed."

We either embrace Jesus entirely as God, Lord, and Savior, or we choose our own way by identifying Him as but one of many well-meaning religious leaders. The choice is ours, but the consequences of that choice are beyond our control.

Digging Deeper Into Chapter Nine

"Christians are not supposed to judge!" How I wish I had a dollar for every time I heard that statement. If we think about the concept at its root level, we realize that judging involves forming an opinion about someone or something. We all do it. Every day. For example, I judge chocolate–peanut butter ice cream from our local shop to be better than the pumpkin ice cream (that never melted) some friends and I purchased from a convenience store while on a fishing trip.

When it comes to people, judging becomes more nuanced. If I am choosing which employee to promote, which contractor to hire, or which concert to attend, I cannot help but make judgments. But if I judge a wealthy person as worthy of more honor than a common laborer, I have entered dangerous spiritual territory.

The environment of the garden of Eden was not judgmental, but relational. However, when Adam and Eve disobeyed God's command by eating from the tree of the knowledge of good and evil, they propelled humanity into new and unpleasant territory.

Eating from the forbidden tree made our ancient parents *aware* not only of standards of good and evil, but also of good and bad in general. Sadly, we have all inherited those tendencies. This awareness ever colors our interactions with one another. Living by law-based moral standards (i.e., legalism) especially breeds judgmental attitudes, and so we measure people, including ourselves, in light of others.

This is where the concept of *righteousness* enters the picture. Simply put, a righteous person is someone who meets expected standards. Of course, we can think about righteousness from a kingdom of God perspective (i.e., kingdom righteousness), but there is also a social element to the concept. The socially righteous are those who seem to live up to the often-changing social standards related to appearance, performance, and wealth. We call the socially unrighteous all kinds of names such as "loser," "chump," and "moron," to name a few.

The judgmental attitudes condemned by the Bible find their roots in pride. As we compare ourselves to others, we either lift up or put down. We elevate others to celebrity status or we look down at them as the dregs of society.

Dig deeper: James 2:1–9

This might be difficult for some to accept, but God does not view people with the judgmental mindsets common to humanity. Nor has it ever been His desire to judge us. Judgmentalism is the product of human choices.

The Lord gave the Mosaic law with its many commands to show the futility of living under law-based standards. Because law breeds judgment, He allowed ancient Israel to experience the painful consequences of their choices. But God always had His eye on a greater goal, a new type of living. And He used the futility of legalism to stir our hearts for something better. Christ's new covenant of grace is that better way. Law and judgment, or grace and life; the choice is ours.

See also: Jeremiah 31:31–34
2 Corinthians 3:5–9
Galatians 3:19–28

QUESTIONS

1. Why is it foolish to say Jesus never existed?
2. What is the problem with thinking God the Father differs in character from God the Son?
3. How does the law of Moses relate to the tree of the knowledge of good and evil?
4. Why does living by law breed judgment?
5. What was the primary purpose of the Mosaic law?
6. How does the new covenant in Christ differ from the old covenant law under Moses?

Chapter 10

The Redemptive Power of the Cross

As I waited in a grocery store line, a woman attempted to buy a large number of snack bars, but her debit card would not work. I had the money and could have helped out, but I hesitated. Was it really a good purchase for her? I questioned whether they were any more nutritious than cigarettes. Just as she was about to go to her car to look for money, the woman behind me stepped up and volunteered to pay for the order. Tears began to flow as the older lady cried with appreciation.

I felt pretty bad for my lack of generosity. If no one else had stepped up, I probably would have left the store feeling little remorse, but the loving example of another exposed my shortcomings. And so I drove home, berating myself for the hesitancy, for squandering an opportunity to show God's love to someone in need.

If only that was the only time I have felt self-condemned! I could mention many more personal failures—all of which make my heart deeply grateful for the cross.

How do you attempt to resolve a moral failure? Do you blame others to justify yourself? Do you do good deeds to atone for the bad? Do you let the guilt accumulate until it becomes a burden too heavy to bear? Do you harden your heart to alleviate feelings of guilt?

THE CROSS CHANGES EVERYTHING

The cross of Jesus Christ changes everything. Through the cross, we can find forgiveness for our sins, the removal of guilt and condemnation, and even the eradication of shame. Through the cross, we are spiritually reborn, our relationship with God is restored, and the Holy Spirit comes to dwell in our hearts. Through the cross, the curse of sin is broken and the blessings of God are released.

The power of the cross lies outside ourselves. I have seen religious pride up close and personal, and there is nothing God-honoring about it. Pride led to the Pharisees' downfall, and it persists even today among devout church attenders. But as we grasp the meaning of the cross and the depths of God's plan for salvation, everything changes. Through faith, we can reap the benefits of Christ's sacrificial death, but it provides no platform for self-righteous boasting.

THE ROAD TO THE CROSS

When the heavenly Father surveyed humanity and its broken state, He could find no one to remedy the situation. And so He sent His beloved Son. Conceived of the Holy Spirit and born to a virgin, Jesus became God *incarnate*—that is, God in human flesh. Jesus lived in perfect obedience to the heavenly Father's will, fulfilled every requirement of the Mosaic law, and walked in complete humility. Pride is a core root of our human sinfulness, but Jesus was not beguiled by its deceptive influence. Both fully God and fully man, He lived a sinless existence. But Jesus was born to die as the "Lamb of God."

As the Lord prepared to deliver the ancient Israelites from Egypt, He instituted the *Passover* celebration. The people of Israel were commanded to spread the blood of a lamb around the doorposts of their homes so the angel of death would pass over their households. The firstborn sons of Egypt suffered a terrible fate as a consequence of their rebellion against God, but the people of Israel were spared.

After Israel's exodus from Egypt, Passover lambs were sacrificed *annually*. Perfect, innocent lambs were slain so human sins could be temporarily forgiven. Scripture tells us that the life found in innocent blood atones for the death and corruption of sin (Leviticus 17:11). The custom might repulse some people, but the greater repulsion comes from the effect vile human sinfulness has in the nostrils of God. Alas, those who offend their Creator are often unaware (Revelation 3:14–22).

If all this sounds extreme, that is because it is. If we think about what transpired in Eden, Adam and Eve committed treason against the most benevolent government ever to exist. And we, through pride, have inherited those same treasonous desires. That is why the Bible teaches that humans are natural enemies of God (Romans 5:10).

I do not think we are opposed to the concept of God—as long as it conforms to our desires. We generally want a greater Being who gives meaning to life, provides a sense of security, and instills hope for the future. But when it comes to a sovereign King who rules over the universe and commands obedience, we hesitate. We are okay with a "god" who conforms to our image, but that is not how reality works. The kingdom of God draws near only as we yield to our true Creator.

THE POWER OF THE BLOOD

The blood of innocent lambs played a vital role in covering human sin, but that was never the Lord's permanent plan. He wanted something more powerful and longer lasting, a way to transform human hearts rather than temporary measures to be repeated year after year.

When John the Baptist saw Jesus coming to be water baptized, he declared, "Behold, the Lamb of God who takes away the sin of the world!" (John 1:29b). Jesus was crucified at the time of the Passover, further confirming the purpose of His death (1 Corinthians 5:7).

The cross was God's plan from the very beginning. Several hundred years before Jesus walked this earth, the prophet Isaiah proclaimed:

> Yet He Himself bore our sicknesses,
> and He carried our pains;
> but we in turn regarded Him stricken,
> struck down by God, and afflicted.
> But He was pierced because of our transgressions,
> crushed because of our iniquities;
> punishment for our peace was on Him,
> and we are healed by His wounds.
> We all went astray like sheep;
> we all have turned to our own way;
> and the LORD has punished Him
> for the iniquity of us all.
> Isaiah 53:4–6 (HCSB)

Isaiah continued, saying, "The Lord was pleased to crush Him, putting Him to grief; if He would render Himself as a guilt offering." (Isaiah

53:10). God does not have a cruel streak; He was looking beyond the cross to see His relationship with humanity restored.

Until Jesus came to earth, people could only approach God from a distance. His manifest presence dwelt within the confines of an elaborate temple in a 30' x 30' x 30' room called the "Holy of Holies." Isolating the Holy of Holies was a four-inch-thick curtain (veil) meant to keep everyone distant. To enter God's holy presence without being cleansed from sin would have spelled certain death.

As Jesus breathed His last, the veil of the temple split in two from top to bottom (Matthew 27:50–51). The Creator of everything was giving *all* people an opportunity to access His presence. And just as importantly, the manifest presence of the Holy Spirit could now dwell in diverse human hearts. This amazing opportunity was made possible by the sacrificial blood of Jesus, which has the power to cleanse every sin, no matter how vile.

That the temple was torn from top to bottom communicates yet another vital message: the action came from heaven to earth. Humanity was not forcing itself into God's presence. Instead, the Lord was the *initiator,* providing sacrificial blood to cleanse our sins so we might be made holy and draw near to Him.

The New Testament often uses the term "saints" (Romans 1:7; Jude 1:3). Some people mistakenly believe it is a status to be earned. That is how humanity thinks, but it is not what the Bible teaches. To be a saint is to be a holy person of God—one who has been cleansed by the power of Jesus' blood. If you cannot accept God's ability to forgive your sins, you think more highly of your failures than of Christ's blood.

The Lord created humans to live, but we died because of disobedience. Jesus was born to die as a sacrifice for our sins in obedience to the Father's desire, but death could not hold Him.

What does all this mean? *Your Creator wants you*—and in a good way! It does not matter where you came from or where you have been. It does not matter whether you have a history of religious observance or have left a long trail of moral failures. Christ's blood supersedes all!

The ultimate purpose of Jesus' sacrifice was for us to be forgiven and cleansed. Through the redemptive power of the cross, God has provided an amazing opportunity for you to draw near. Will you?

Digging Deeper
Into Chapter Ten

Before becoming a Christian, I regarded Jesus as nothing more than a noble religious leader who died for the benefit of others. Worshiping Him as the Son of God seemed both bizarre and unwarranted. My perspective is now very different, but many others continue to question why millions of Christians would bend their knees in prayer and lift their arms in worship. Thankfully, the Bible has much to say in this regard.

More than any other title, Jesus referred to Himself as the "Son of Man." The connection to Adam and humanity is obvious, but it also has *Messianic* roots, speaking of God's chosen instrument to establish the kingdom of heaven on earth. According to the prophet Daniel:

> "I kept looking in the night visions,
> And behold, with the clouds of heaven
> One like a Son of Man was coming,
> And He came up to the Ancient of Days
> And was presented before Him.
> "And to Him was given dominion,
> Glory and a kingdom,
> That all the peoples, nations and men of every language
> Might serve Him.
> His dominion is an everlasting dominion
> Which will not pass away;
> And His kingdom is one
> Which will not be destroyed."
> Daniel 7:13–14

This passage points toward the coming Christ—the Messiah of God sent to bring the kingdom of heaven to earth. But we sometimes struggle to grasp its full significance because Jesus walked so humbly during His time on earth. And while it is true that He never coveted the glory of humanity, the Bible provides powerful indicators of Christ's full identity.

> *Dig deeper: Matthew 26:59–66*
> *Matthew 28:18*

Not only did the religious leaders get the message of Jesus' identity, so did Christ's followers. Their writings clearly exalt Him above all others.

> *Dig deeper: Ephesians 1:15–23*
> *Philippians 2:1–11*

The belief in Jesus Christ's deity has persisted since the earliest days of the Christian faith. Discovered by an inmate under the floor of a prison, the 16' x 32' *Megiddo Mosaic* dates back to about AD 230.[1] Once the floor of a Christian worship hall, the mosaic identifies Jesus as God. Both historical and archaeological records consistently affirm that Christians have always honored Jesus as divine.

I do not know which is more amazing—Jesus' identity as both the Son of God and Son of Man, or His humility. Our Savior did not seek glory, but He stands worthy of all glory and honor and praise!

QUESTIONS

1. What makes Jesus unique compared to all the other religious leaders throughout history?
2. What would Christianity be without the cross?
3. How does the cross of Christ affect our human potential to boast?
4. What is significant about the veil of the temple tearing in two from top to bottom?
5. What makes the blood of Jesus powerful enough to cleanse all our sins?
6. Why is it a statement of faith and not pride to say Christians are saints in the eyes of God?

---

1. "The Megiddo Mosaic," *Bible History Daily* (blog), Biblical Archaeology Society, November 13, 2024, accessed February 20, 2025, https://www.biblicalarchaeology.org/exhibits-events/the-megiddo-mosaic/.

Chapter 11

An Eye on the Veil

I once watched a disturbing video concerning a man who died horrifically in an electrical accident because he had ignored safety protocols. Not fully comprehending the situation, the unfortunate fellow tried to measure a 2,300-volt electrical current with a meter that could not nearly handle the capacity. The connection created an electrical arc, which led to an explosion. A ball of fire then flew from the equipment into his unprotected face. The aftermath was not pretty. Sadly, the man had grown too comfortable with his working environment and had lost respect for the power involved.

We could say something similar about how people view our Creator. When considering a conversation about God, a person might envision sitting on a coffee-shop couch, sipping a warm latte, and nibbling on a piece of fresh biscotti. Throughout the discussion, the individual would be tempted to embrace "palatable" Christian truths while rejecting those he or she does not like. We could compare the experience to dining at a buffet restaurant. But do we grasp the reality of the Almighty God? Our cosmos provides but a small taste.

Have you ever sat too long in the sun? Unfortunately, I have had more than one painful sunburn—enough for me to lather my face, arms, and legs with SPF 10,000 lotion when I go out on my kayak. And we are ninety-three million miles from just an average-sized star. Some are a hundred times larger.

Now imagine climbing into a spaceship to visit the sun—although only in the world of fiction would such an idea be considered. Our solar system contains forces almost beyond our ability to fathom. And this is just our small collection of heavenly bodies.

We could also consider the Milky Way Galaxy or the hundreds of billions of other galaxies—nobody knows for sure how many—beyond that. Ours is a universe of uncharted power. And while we struggle to grasp the scope of our cosmos, God simply *spoke* it all into existence.

GOD'S HOLINESS

Coming in contact with the Lord's unfiltered holiness might be like being suspended not in an elegant moonbeam, but an intense bolt of lightning. Add to the mix the corruption of human sin, and the experience would be worse than any we could ever imagine. The concept is mysterious, but God's purity is so extreme that we might compare it to the intensity of high voltage electricity.

Four brief accounts from the Bible help provide an invaluable perspective. The first involves God's visit with the people of Israel on Mt. Sinai after He delivered them from slavery in Egypt. This was when the Ten Commandments were given:

> Now Mount Sinai was all in smoke because the LORD descended upon it in fire; and its smoke ascended like the smoke of a furnace, and the whole mountain quaked violently. When the sound of the trumpet grew louder and louder, Moses spoke and God answered him with thunder. Exodus 19:18–19

> All the people perceived the thunder and the lightning flashes and the sound of the trumpet and the mountain smoking; and when the people saw it, they trembled and stood at a distance. Then they said to Moses, "Speak to us yourself and we will listen; but let not God speak to us, or we will die." Exodus 20:18–19

Next we read of the prophet Isaiah's intense encounter with the Lord. Here was a spokesperson for God recognizing the grave danger of his situation:

> In the year of King Uzziah's death I saw the LORD sitting on a throne, lofty and exalted, with the train of His robe filling the temple. Seraphim stood above Him, each having six wings: with two he covered his face, and with two he covered his feet, and with two he flew. And one called out to another and said,

> "Holy, Holy, Holy, is the Lord of hosts,
> The whole earth is full of His glory."
>
> And the foundations of the thresholds trembled at the voice of him who called out, while the temple was filling with smoke. Then I said,
>
> "Woe is me, for I am ruined!
> Because I am a man of unclean lips,
> And I live among a people of unclean lips;
> For my eyes have seen the King, the Lord of hosts."
> Isaiah 6:1–5

Now, we move to the New Testament, and specifically, an account by the apostle John in the Book of Revelation:

> Then I turned to see the voice that was speaking with me. And having turned I saw seven golden lampstands; and in the middle of the lampstands I saw one like a son of man, clothed in a robe reaching to the feet, and girded across His chest with a golden sash. His head and His hair were white like white wool, like snow; and His eyes were like a flame of fire. His feet were like burnished bronze, when it has been made to glow in a furnace, and His voice was like the sound of many waters. In His right hand He held seven stars, and out of His mouth came a sharp two-edged sword; and His face was like the sun shining in its strength.
>
> When I saw Him, I fell at His feet like a dead man. Revelation 1:12–17a

Remember, this is the same John who leaned on Jesus' breast during the Last Supper. But here, seeing the Lord in His unfiltered glory, one of Jesus' best friends could not even stand.

Finally, we look at Christ's return to earth for His Second Coming:

> And I saw heaven opened, and behold, a white horse, and He who sat on it is called Faithful and True, and in righteousness

He judges and wages war.... From His mouth comes a sharp sword, so that with it He may strike down the nations, and He will rule them with a rod of iron; and He treads the wine press of the fierce wrath of God, the Almighty. And on His robe and on His thigh He has a name written, "KING OF KINGS, AND LORD OF LORDS." Revelation 19:11, 15–16

Only the foolish would treat the teachings of the Almighty God like a buffet meal!

HOLY LOVE

The Lord visited the people of Israel because He wanted them near. But they could not handle the intensity of His presence. And so He enacted a series of rituals, mainly involving the sacrificial blood of innocent animals, to allow the people to be close without being destroyed.

God also confined the manifestation of His presence to the Holy of Holies. It was here that His presence dwelt for centuries. But only one person was permitted within that sacred space. It was the Jewish high priest who could enter only once each year—on the Day of Atonement—with sacrificial blood for the cleansing of human sins. The life in that blood was enough to cover the death-permeated transgressions of the people for a limited time (Leviticus 17:11).

Long did the Lord keep His eye on the temple veil, treasuring a deep desire to be nearer to humanity. It was not something God needed for Himself as much as an expression of His deep love for us.

When Jesus breathed His last, when the sacrificial blood of the eternal Passover Lamb had fulfilled its purpose, God tore the thick veil of the temple from top to bottom. Fifty days later, He poured out His Spirit that He might dwell within human hearts forever (Acts 2:1–18).

Because of the blood of Jesus, and only because of the blood of Jesus, we have an opportunity to be near to our Creator in ways beyond imagination—and without being terrified. But let us not fool ourselves into thinking we could ever enter that holy presence by any means other than the precious blood of the eternal Lamb of God.

Digging Deeper
Into Chapter Eleven

Christians consider the Bible to be *one book* composed of two parts: the Old Testament and the New Testament. The Old Testament, also known as the Hebrew Bible, provides an account of creation and then focuses on the story of Abraham and his descendants.

As part of His plan to redeem humanity, the Lord established a special *covenant* relationship with Abraham. That covenant continued through Abraham's son Jacob, whom God renamed *Israel*. It was to this group of people, the Jews, that God gave the Mosaic law.

The Jews expressed confidence in their ability to obey the laws communicated by Moses (Exodus 19:8; 24:3, 7), but they failed miserably. Of course, God knew this would happen, but giving them an opportunity to fulfill their boast was part of His plan for redemption.

As the nation of Israel failed repeatedly to honor the Lord's commands, He began to direct their attention to a *new* and *better* covenant—one He established through the person of Jesus Christ.

While the Old Testament mostly addressed the *physical* descendants of Abraham, the New Testament focuses on Abraham's *spiritual* descendants who become part of God's covenant family through faith in Jesus Christ (Galatians 3:7).

The relationship between the Old and New Testaments is powerful, and without the Old, we would be hard-pressed to understand much about the New. In particular, we find physical "types" throughout the Old Testament that help to illuminate the greater spiritual realities of the new covenant. One such type is found in the story of *Esther*.

God exalted the Jewish woman Esther to become the Queen of Persia at about the time a wicked government official named Haman was plotting to destroy the Jews. The situation was dire, and Esther's cousin

Mordecai exhorted her to appeal to the king for help. But to approach the king without being summoned was to risk death. After the Jews fasted and prayed for three days, Esther summoned the courage to approach King Ahasuerus. The monarch extended his golden scepter to welcome the young woman into his presence, saving the Jewish people from destruction.

Dig deeper: Esther 5:1–3

The story of Esther illuminates a greater spiritual reality about approaching the God of heaven. Though our Creator is fearsome in so many ways, through the new covenant in Christ, He has extended His golden scepter of favor to you and me.

We can confidently approach God through prayer, leaning into His favor and the profound privilege we have been given. And when our time on earth ends, as we all know it will, we will have the honor of approaching His heavenly throne without terror, or even anxiety.

To fear God, in a healthy sense, means to *revere* Him as the Lord and Creator of all things. But, thankfully, we need not keep our distance. Jesus died as a sacrifice for our sins so we can draw near to heaven's eternal King. God knows everything about us but still wants to draw us into His presence through the sacrificial blood of Jesus Christ. Amazing!

See also: Matthew 27:50–54
Romans 5:1–11
Hebrews 4:12–16

QUESTIONS

1. What other physical "types" from the Old Testament help us better understand the spiritual reality of the New?
2. What makes God fearsome?
3. What does it mean to have a healthy fear of God?
4. Why is it foolish to treat the Word of God like a buffet meal?
5. What does it mean to you that God wants you near to Him?
6. Why can we approach the Lord's presence with confidence?

Chapter 12
Born Anew

I fell in love with science at a young age. I remember my fifth-grade teacher helping me create an experiment because I questioned something he said in class. Later, after cultivating my scientific interests throughout high school, I enrolled as a chemistry major at a state university. That experience opened up yet another world of learning.

About midway through my sophomore year, I was introduced to the Bible and challenged to more seriously consider the Christian faith. I cannot say I was actively pursuing a deeper understanding of my existence at the time; I was mostly looking for a happier, more comfortable lifestyle with a somewhat meaningful career. But a mysterious change was beginning to take place within me.

Several months later, I bowed my knee to Christ in submission to His Kingship. Captivated by the teachings of the Bible, I also grew to realize the gulf between science and Christianity was not nearly as wide as I had been led to believe. Science involves a quest to understand our natural world, while my newfound faith focused on the spiritual reality around us. One realm is mostly visible, and the other unseen, but similar principles of discovery transcend the two. Both require an *objective* pursuit of truth.

After graduating from college, I spent fifteen-plus years working in a coal laboratory. I had considered pursuing scientific research, but the coal lab was local. My life vision had shifted, and I became more interested in serving God through Christian ministry than in pursuing science as a vocation.

CONVERSATIONS ABOUT FAITH

During those lab years, I started serving with a campus ministry at the same university from which I had graduated. Working with college students proved to be richly rewarding, albeit highly challenging. I cannot begin to tell you how many conversations I had with students and educators about God and the nature of life, but several of those discussions have stayed with me throughout the years.

One older student did not want to accept the Christian faith as real, but struggled with the Old Testament prophecies regarding Jesus. He could not deny the supernatural nature of those documented prophecies. Another student believed Christianity to be true, but a close non-Christian friend had recently died. The young man could not bear the idea of her being eternally lost, and so he chose to shut down any thoughts about becoming a Christian himself. How painful!

A third conversation still haunts me. A young man had read through the New Testament with genuine interest, but recoiled at the high moral standards Jesus presented in His Sermon on the Mount (see Matthew 5). He felt it impossible to live up to those standards, and decided that life would be more tolerable if he rejected Christianity entirely. Try as I might to help him see a different perspective, he walked away seemingly unchanged. What a barrier human wisdom can create between us and our Creator!

EYES FOR THE KINGDOM

One of the best-known verses of the Bible can be found in the third chapter of John's gospel:

> "For God so loved the world, that He gave His only begotten Son, that whoever believes in Him shall not perish, but have eternal life." John 3:16

Jesus was speaking with Nicodemus, a Pharisee, who came to speak with the Lord under the cover of darkness. Many of the Pharisees were taking offense to Jesus' bold statements, but Nicodemus could not deny the hand of God at work through Christ's many miracles. It was during this discussion that the Son of God sent Nicodemus' mind racing:

> Jesus answered and said to him, "Truly, truly, I say to you, unless one is born again he cannot see the kingdom of God." John 3:3

Born Anew

The Greek word *anothen* has multiple meanings. We could translate it as "again," as in starting over. And it can also mean "from above," as from a higher place.[1] By his response, Nicodemus took it to mean "again," and struggled to understand the concept. But the latter part of the Lord's statement also speaks an important message. Without being born again, or born from above, a person cannot see the kingdom of God. What does this statement mean?

Remembering that the Bible is a unified book composed of sixty-six different parts, we think back to God's warning in the second chapter of Genesis:

> The LORD God commanded the man, saying, "From any tree of the garden you may eat freely; but from the tree of the knowledge of good and evil you shall not eat, for in the day that you eat from it you will surely die." Genesis 2:16–17

The breath of Adam and Eve did not suddenly expire as they took their curious first bite of the forbidden fruit. But they did die spiritually because their union with God was severed. Independence is what they sought, and independence is what they got. Tragically, the first humans recognized the consequences the instant their spiritual world went suddenly dark! No spiritual life. No spiritual sight. No meaningful connection to the God who had so lovingly created them. But thankfully, from the very beginning, God had a plan to redeem humanity from its spiritually lost state.

REBIRTH

Coming to the Son of God under the cover of nightfall, Nicodemus—a teacher of Jewish law—was being challenged to consider the spiritual nature of God's redemptive process. Jesus was not coming as an earthly king to establish a human government; He was introducing a *spiritual kingdom* that exists on a higher plane than anything we know. And to grasp the nature of that kingdom, Nicodemus would need to be spiritually reborn. Natural eyes will forever remain blind to God's ways.

---

1. Spiros Zodhiates, *The Complete Word Study Dictionary: New Testament* (Chattanooga, TN: AMG Publishers, 2000).

The Bible diverges here from most other religious teachings. So much of religious life involves trying to become improved versions of ourselves. Seeking to put our moral failures in the past, we take new steps of pious devotion, doing our best to live up to each respective standard. But God's plan unfolds differently. Instead of becoming better versions of ourselves, we are *reborn* through the power of the Holy Spirit. Being reborn means becoming a *new creation* in Christ:

> Therefore from now on we recognize no one according to the flesh; even though we have known Christ according to the flesh, yet now we know Him in this way no longer. Therefore if anyone is in Christ, he is a new creature; the old things passed away; behold, new things have come. 2 Corinthians 5:16–17

I did not grow a halo when I first surrendered my life to the Lord, olives did not suddenly become my favorite food, and the ability to play a harp did not displace my nonexistent sense of rhythm. But something *within me* changed! My heart had been reborn, and I began to view life through a different lens.

It was at this point that God made me spiritually alive, freeing me from the dominion of the devil to become a citizen of His glorious kingdom (Colossians 1:13). Suddenly, I could relate to my Creator in a way I never knew possible. And really, knowing God has always been the essence of eternal life (John 17:3). New desires, imparted from heaven, also began to form in my heart.

This new birth in Christ can happen to both young and old, but it *must* happen if we are to relate to our Creator in any meaningful way. We are changed as we cease living out of a sense of obligation and embrace a newfound desire to love God and do His will. The change comes from *within* rather than being imposed upon us by external requirements. Our part is not to labor for God's favor, but to *respond* to what Jesus has already accomplished on our behalf.

What profound, amazing news! Through the new covenant in Christ, we can move beyond the burdensome requirements of moral and religious perfection, free to live with hearts that beat to an eternal rhythm.

Digging Deeper Into Chapter Twelve

Have you ever experienced *thymic involution*? If you are beyond puberty, you likely have. The thymus is a small gland in the middle of the chest that produces T cells to help the immune system function properly. Once a child hits puberty, fatty tissue begins to replace the thymus, and the shrinking process is called thymic involution.

Medical experts once thought the thymus was an anomaly of human evolution, that it no longer serves a useful purpose. They also suspected an enlarged thymus to be the cause of unexplained infant deaths. And so they began to treat an enlarged thymus with X-rays.

To make the X-ray treatments easier, a child would sometimes be placed on its mother's unprotected lap. And so it was that both mother and child could be afflicted by cancer from large doses of radiation.

The medical professionals involved with these treatments were intelligent and well-intentioned experts. But because of their limited knowledge at the time, they did not recognize the tragic consequences of their misguided efforts. Terrible suffering resulted.

Similarly, just because a religious leader has a lofty title or sports a religious studies degree, does not mean that person can see and understand the dynamics of God's eternal kingdom. Such abilities come only from a new-birth experience facilitated by the Holy Spirit.

The Pharisees were likely the most-educated religious leaders of their day, and yet Jesus called them "blind guides of the blind" (Matthew 15:14). In fact, they were the ones who manipulated people and circumstances to have the Son of God crucified.

Spiritual insight does not come from a school or religious organization; we can see spiritually only as the Holy Spirit opens our eyes and illuminates our minds to understand the teachings of the Bible.

So, how do we know which religious leaders to trust as we seek to better understand God and His ways? While I cannot give you a foolproof formula regarding whom to trust, I can provide three helpful tips.

To begin, we ask if the individual esteems the Bible as the *inspired*, *infallible*, and *authoritative* Word of God. While we can sometimes disagree regarding the exact teachings of the Bible, those who fail to honor it as the standard for spiritual truth will also fail to accurately discern the ways of the Lord.

See also: 2 Timothy 3:10–17

Next, we must ask whether the person has a firm grasp on the Biblical doctrine of *grace*. While we cannot identify a single secret to victorious spiritual living, the Christian life does not work apart from grace.

Dig deeper: Romans 5:15–21

A third key involves considering the *spiritual fruit* of a leader's life. No one is perfect; this we must accept. Even the most esteemed leaders will have faults and flaws. But are they humble? Do they consider themselves *servants* of God and humanity? Are they willing to submit to others in authority? Are their lives characterized by abundant, sweet spiritual fruit? We do not want to be overly critical, but neither should we align ourselves with false teachers. Let us take care to connect with those humble leaders who are truly servants of our most-high King.

Dig deeper: Matthew 7:15–23
Acts 20:17–32

QUESTIONS

1. What does it mean to be born again, and why is it necessary?
2. What does it mean to become a new creation in Christ?
3. Why do we need spiritual insight to see God's kingdom?
4. Why is a leader's view of the Bible of the utmost importance?
5. Why is an accurate understanding of grace so important?
6. What are some markers of a humble, spiritually fruitful leader?

Chapter 13
With Open Eyes

"Somebody needs to get yelled at!" I blurted to the young cashier who was doing a not-so-good job of explaining the consequences of bad online reviews. Very much displeased at that moment on a warm Saturday morning, I had been asking about the best way to complain about a lack of clear pricing at our local home improvement store. For the second time in as many visits, I had loaded my cart with wood only to discover the cost did not match my expectations. In this case, the display price was about two-thirds the actual price.

"This isn't rocket science," I stewed to myself on the drive home. "With such inflated prices, I should be able to clearly identify the cost of any item. How else can I make informed decisions?" I then breathed a sigh of gratitude that I had restrained my anger and not disrespected the young man. But I did go home and respond to the retailer's request to complete a survey. My review was not favorable.

With spiritual matters, it can appear as though we lack clear markers when trying to understand what is true. Some disillusioned people have even given "negative reviews" about God's plan. The situation is not as bad as it might appear, though, and the Lord certainly is not to blame. Let us consider some of what He has provided for us:

- **The Created Universe** - Modern technology allows us to see the heavens like never before, and projects such as the James Webb Space Telescope have not disappointed. The immense, captivating expanse of our cosmos extends far beyond our imaginations, challenging us to explain even its existence. And within our small sphere of earth, we find a complexity of life just as dazzling. Random? No way! Our Creator has provided us with tangible evidence of His existence through the material world around us.

- **The Bible** - The Bible is far more than a religious text espousing mystical concepts; it is a gift from our Creator providing an opportunity for us to draw near to Him. And we have already shown that the Bible's credibility stands out among religious documents.

- **Jesus** - God Himself came to earth that we might know Him and His ways. Christ's radical lifestyle revealed the reality of heaven's goodness, while His resurrection from the dead created a new beginning for humanity.

- **Witnesses** - Contemporaries of Jesus have provided us with eyewitness accounts of His life and actions. And beyond that, followers of Christ testify regularly of God's goodness and how He has transformed their lives and relationships.

Recognizing God's provision might not eliminate all confusion, but it does help us realize the lengths to which the Lord has gone on our behalf. If we have a problem grasping the spiritual reality around us, our Creator is not to blame. But if God is not to blame, who is?

THE DEVIL

Some people scoff at the idea of the devil's existence. But the Bible records a face-to-face encounter Jesus had with "old slewfoot" during a time of weakness as He fasted in the wilderness (Matthew 4:1–11). According to Jesus, the devil is both a liar and a murderer (John 8:44).

Take a minute to imagine the grand opening of the home improvement store mentioned above. High-ranking company officials and local dignitaries gather to celebrate the opening with great fanfare. New customers stroll across sparkling floors and past pristine displays adorned with perfect signage. On that day, you would have had no trouble identifying the cost of virtually any item.

Now picture an unscrupulous business owner who has a stranglehold on the local home improvement market. How would such a person react to the new competition? Not well. And so the man sets about to sabotage the new store. Working his way through the building in unassuming fashion, he quietly switches the display pricing. Expensive items suddenly appear cheap, and inexpensive items command absurd prices. In some places, he removes the pricing entirely. If complacent workers fail to correct the errors, what will the store be like after a few weeks? Welcome to the world in which we live!

The devil's deep hatred for God compels him to seek humanity's demise through deception. Confused by the "price tags" around them, people waste their lives on things with no lasting value. An unfortunate example would be a man who sacrifices his family to pursue success, fame, or wealth, only to realize at death how convoluted his priorities had been.

OURSELVES

I wish I could say the devil was our only problem, but pride also blinds us. Adam and Eve ate from the forbidden fruit, thinking it would make them wise. And though their eyes were opened to standards of good and evil, they were also closed to God's wisdom. Speaking through the prophet Isaiah, our Creator made this reality clear:

> Seek the LORD while He may be found;
> Call upon Him while He is near.
> Let the wicked forsake his way
> And the unrighteous man his thoughts;
> And let him return to the LORD,
> And He will have compassion on him,
> And to our God,
> For He will abundantly pardon.
> "For My thoughts are not your thoughts,
> Nor are your ways My ways," declares the LORD.
> "For as the heavens are higher than the earth,
> So are My ways higher than your ways
> And My thoughts than your thoughts."
> Isaiah 55:6–9

Though painful to admit, we do not naturally understand the spiritual realm because we view life on a different plane from God. Such spiritual blindness results from human choices exploited by evil forces.

As an example, people are naturally appearance oriented. Men tend to objectify women, and women judge themselves and others by how they look. Society then creates a hierarchy based on outward beauty, with the "winners" becoming popular and even wealthy, while the losers slink into the world of "wannabes."

It does not seem fair to relegate people to obscurity—or public ridicule—because they do not meet the ever-changing standards of prevailing human opinion. Some genuine and sincere souls have suffered terribly from genetic influences over which they had no control. How could a loving God allow such injustice?

Through the Bible, we discover the problem lies not with God, but with our natural human quest to measure up to outward standards:

> But the LORD said to Samuel, "Do not look at his appearance or at the height of his stature, because I have rejected him; for God sees not as man sees, for man looks at the outward appearance, but the LORD looks at the heart." 1 Samuel 16:7

God's plan is good and beautiful and without confusion. But our human drive to pursue independence has distorted our perspectives.

SIMPLE BUT PROFOUND

John Wesley—founder of the Methodist Church—helped set the standard for religious devotion while attending Oxford University. He even became a missionary, and in 1735 boarded a ship bound for the new-world colony of Georgia. But Wesley had no peace. Resting on the faulty foundation of religious devotion, he had spent years apart from God while supposedly in His service. Only after that painful experience would Wesley actually exercise faith in Christ for salvation.

The gospel is simple and yet profound. But we will be blind to its reality if we do not humble our hearts and look to the Lord for wisdom. How many people—even religious ones—have gone to their graves lacking an understanding of the good news of the kingdom because they never took the time to press into God for wisdom? Our loving Father wants us to know, so let us not waste the amazing opportunity before us!

Digging Deeper
Into Chapter Thirteen

Some people profess to have a secret special knowledge of God's ways. Others claim it is impossible for us to know anything about the Almighty. Both groups fall into error by taking statements of truth in directions never intended by our Creator.

Yes, it is true we can know nothing about the spiritual Being we call "God" unless He allows us to. But as already seen, the Creator of our cosmos has gone to great lengths to provide a witness on our behalf. Still, our ability to know the Lord and His ways should never be considered automatic. We can learn much in this regard from Matthew 13, which tells of the Parable of the Sower.

Dig deeper: Matthew 13:3-23

I am particularly struck by Christ's dialogue with his disciples:

> And Jesus answered them, "To you it has been granted to know the mysteries of the kingdom of heaven, but to them it has not been granted." Matthew 13:11

Does this statement confirm that God reveals His ways only to an elite few who have been selected for the special privilege of knowing Him? Not at all. But we must consider the context.

Jesus made a contrast between His disciples and the crowds following Him. The crowds recognized something special in the self-professed Son of Man. And so, in large numbers, they looked to Him for healing from physical ailments and freedom from demonic oppression. But the crowds did not follow Jesus the way His disciples did.

The disciples—and there were more than just the twelve—sought to know Christ to the point of sacrifice. They were willing to pay a steep price to be in His presence, and they took deliberate steps of obedience in response to His teachings. In other words, the crowds wanted something from Jesus, but the disciples sought Jesus Himself. So, while it is true that God does not scatter His wisdom indiscriminately, He has also opened the door wide to those who genuinely want to know Him.

Dig deeper: Proverbs 2:1-9
Jeremiah 29:11-13
James 1:1-8

Anyone can develop a deeper understanding of God's ways as long as efforts are made according to His design. That means admitting our need, and making genuine efforts to search His Word and pray for wisdom. It also means softening our hearts by letting go of the stubborn self-will and welcoming His kingship. And, just as importantly, we must believe He will answer—without partiality—our requests for wisdom.

Perhaps the most important key of all is to recognize the Holy Spirit as the One who opens our eyes and illuminates heaven's truth. The Spirit of God will use a multitude of means—such as pastors, teachers, and authors—but *He* always remains the source above them all.

How do we know if we are on the right track? The "fruit" of our beliefs will become increasingly evident. The process of gaining wisdom from heaven might be challenging at times, but it is always good.

Dig deeper: James 3:13-18

QUESTIONS

1. In what ways are people blind to God's truth?
2. Why is it a mistake to think we can know nothing about God?
3. Why is it a mistake to think the Lord gives wisdom only to an exclusive number of spiritually elite leaders?
4. What keeps people blind to God's ways?
5. How has the devil duped you in times past?
6. What means has the Lord provided for us to learn His ways?

Chapter 14

Water Baptism

It was not in a religious setting that I made my decision to become a Christian. I was not responding to a provoking appeal by a pastor or riding on the emotions of inspirational music. I did not raise my hand, step forward to the front of a church, or repeat a "sinner's prayer." I was simply walking back to my college dorm one crisp spring evening after a challenging conversation with a friend.

Regardless of the setting, I knew God was calling me to Himself and my response would come at a price. I cannot explain how, but I instinctively realized that choosing to follow Christ would mean losing some of the most important relationships in my life. After hesitating, I decided that Jesus was worthy of my service no matter the cost.

Looking back, it was as though I had stepped into the current of a mighty river, and the ride has been both exhilarating and frightening. On more than one occasion, I have felt as though I were going to drown. And though I have had the freedom to "come ashore" from the flow of that river at any time, I cannot imagine any other existence. I think Peter said it best when confronted by the types of difficulties we face when following Jesus: "Lord, to whom shall we go? You have words of eternal life. We have believed and have come to know that You are the Holy One of God" (John 6:68b–69).

I had mostly avoided church doors until that point, but began attending regularly and building relationships in the process. The upcoming end of my spring semester meant going home for the summer, so I began considering the options regarding a home church. Attending a Good Friday service at which several local pastors would be speaking seemed like a logical next step.

Five pastors preached sermons that day, but I remember only bits and pieces of one. In it, a pastor expended considerable effort trying to discredit several prophecies about Jesus, so I decided to steer clear of his direction. In the end, I chose a church led by a pastor who had given a message that seemed both Biblical and relevant. And so it was that, midway through the summer, I found myself sitting with a small group of people from the Church of God waiting to be water baptized.

MY BAPTISM

Our church lacked a baptismal tank, which is why we crowded into a fifteen-passenger van and drove to a neighboring community. I did not like the idea of being baptized in a steel tank, but did not feel the choice was mine. I was coming to understand the importance of water baptism, not as a requirement for salvation, but as a vital step of obedience to express newfound faith in Jesus.

On the Day of Pentecost, when the Holy Spirit had been first poured out upon Christ's followers, the apostle Peter delivered a bold message: "Repent, and each of you be baptized in the name of Jesus Christ for the forgiveness of your sins; and you will receive the gift of the Holy Spirit" (Acts 2:38b). Getting water baptized is not something we do just to make our faith more meaningful; it is an act of obedience that reflects a spiritual rebirth.

Some church organizations practice infant baptism, and to a degree, I can understand why. In the early church, entire families would often embrace Christianity together. Even so, infant baptism cannot earn salvation for a person. The ultimate decision to serve God must be made by those who count the cost and grasp the basic ramifications of the choice they are making.

I probably should have been baptized immediately after surrendering my life to the Lord, but I do not remember the opportunity being offered. So when my newfound home church announced an upcoming baptismal service, I knew it was time to act regardless of my personal preferences.

As we sat, with anxious excitement, on a wooden pew in an unfamiliar church building, their pastor approached with a sheepish look. "I'm very sorry," he mumbled, "I forgot to fill the baptismal tank, and it takes several hours. There is no way we can perform water baptisms here this evening."

Disappointed, we all climbed back into the van and headed for home. Along the way, we would be passing a small stream—where I had sometimes skipped school to go fishing—so someone suggested we do the baptisms in a popular swimming hole. It was there, in the flowing waters of the North Branch of the Little Conemaugh River, that I publicly proclaimed my faith in Christ, embracing the sacred new covenant established by Jesus through His blood.

UNDERSTANDING WATER BAPTISM

Water baptism is, in some ways, similar to a *marriage ceremony*. If we think back to the virgin Mary's pregnancy, Joseph, her "betrothed" husband, considered quietly breaking off the union because of perceived infidelity (Matthew 1:18-19). According to the custom of the day, a man and woman would enter a sacred and legal marriage covenant but not sexually consummate the union until a later date. Joseph decided against divorce after an angel informed him Mary had been impregnated by the Holy Spirit to bring the sinless Christ into the world. (I suspect God took this approach because the sinful nature is passed along by the male sperm. I cannot say this with certainty, but imagine that most females would applaud such theology.)

Water baptism resembles a marriage betrothal, involving a public ceremony in which a person proclaims God to be his or her *first love*. Always, love stands at the core of what we do for the Lord. Sometimes, what looks like extreme religious devotion is simply a passionate love relationship between a human and our Almighty Creator.

Water baptism is an *exclusive* act. When I married Debi, I took a vow of exclusivity, meaning I would be faithful to limit my sexual expressions to her alone. Choosing to be water baptized as a follower of Jesus means putting aside all other "gods," whatever form those gods might take.

Water baptism is also a relational act of *trust*. We cannot baptize ourselves but rely upon another person to dip us below the surface of the water. We do this hoping the individual will also lift us out of the water to prevent drowning. Such powerful imagery! As we surrender to God, our old self is buried, our sins are cleansed, and we are raised by Him to a new life in Christ.

Water baptism is also an act of *repentance*. To repent is to change one's mind, which results in changing one's actions. Becoming a citizen of God's kingdom requires embracing the mindsets of His realm. But to do this, we must let go of our own ways, of putting ourselves first.

By choosing to get water baptized we are deciding to live for God and not ourselves. Despite the type of consumerism that seems to characterize modern religion, God does not exist to serve our desires. Jesus died for us, but life is not about us. We exist for Him and His purposes. If the gospel we embrace does not challenge the core of our self-centered thinking, we must question whether it is the real gospel of the kingdom. There can only be one sovereign King in this grand universe, and neither you nor I qualify.

SWEPT UP BY GRACE

My water baptism experience seems representative of my entire Christian life, and perhaps the lives of all Christians. God calls us to let go of control and surrender fully to His will. Such a surrendered lifestyle can feel like death itself, but I always find God's plan to be infinitely better than my own.

Aligning our lives with His design is like stepping into the flow of the mighty river I mentioned previously. We cannot control the path, but the ride is adventurous, life-giving, and rewarding. God's grace is similar. Abounding like water in the ocean, grace favors, empowers, refreshes, and rewards us in ways beyond explanation. But there is one thing grace can never be, and that is subject to our terms. This is a primary lesson proclaimed through water baptism.

Finally, some believers—especially those newer in the faith—will struggle with doubts about whether they are truly Christians. Submitting to the Biblical command to be water baptized helps to minimize such doubts. Water baptism is a deliberate, tangible act of faith. If doubts about whether you are truly saved begin to creep in, remember the decision you made to surrender your life to God, and the way you were washed and raised to a new life in Christ. Our right standing with God always comes through the cross of Jesus Christ, and water baptism helps to remind us of that potent truth.

Digging Deeper Into Chapter Fourteen

The Old Testament book of Hosea is not exactly what I would call normal. It tells the common story of ancient Israel's unfaithfulness to God, but with a unique twist.

Would you believe that God commanded the prophet Hosea to marry a woman who was known for being sexually unfaithful? The Lord did this to illustrate His frustration with Israel's worship of false gods.

Dig deeper: Hosea 1:1-2

The Old Testament describes idolatry as sexual immorality and the worship of false gods as adulterous acts against the Almighty God. I think it is safe to say the issue is one of considerable significance.

What can be more important than how God views His people? While we tend to get caught up with religious protocols, His perspective is *relationship* oriented—so much so that He thinks of us in bride-groom terms.

When the people of ancient Israel worshiped idols, the King of heaven took it personally—as though they were violating the sanctity of a marriage bond. Perhaps that is why the very first of the Ten Commandments stated, "You shall have no other gods before Me."

Dig deeper: Exodus 20:1-3

The Bible bemoans Israel's many lovers, and archaeologists have unearthed large numbers of idols from ancient Israeli homes to confirm those practices. Though heartbroken by their unfaithfulness, as illustrated in Hosea, the Lord always sought to bring them back.

But more than Israel's idolatry, it is God's perspective on the matter that we want to bring to light because it helps us better understand the Christian faith.

While devout people tend to focus on religious practices and rituals, *love* has always been at the center of God's interaction with humanity. He loves us deeply, and He wants us to share the same devotion. *More than anything, becoming a Christian is about falling deeply in love with the God who created us.*

Chapters two and three in the book of Revelation record a series of letters—which were both corrective and encouraging—to seven early churches. The Lord's message to the Ephesian church speaks loudly:

> "I know your deeds and your toil and perseverance, and that you cannot tolerate evil men, and you put to the test those who call themselves apostles, and they are not, and you found them to be false; and you have perseverance and have endured for My name's sake, and have not grown weary. But I have this against you, that you have left your first love. Therefore remember from where you have fallen, and repent and do the deeds you did at first; or else I am coming to you and will remove your lampstand out of its place—unless you repent." Revelation 2:2-5

The church in Ephesus had been faithful in so many ways. And the people had persevered through much adversity. But in the midst of it all, they lost sight of what matters most: love. *More than anything else, the God of heaven wants our hearts.*

> Dig deeper: Matthew 22:34-40
> 1 John 4:15-19

QUESTIONS

1. How does water baptism resemble a marriage betrothal?
2. In what way is water baptism exclusive?
3. What does it mean to repent?
4. Why can grace never be subject to our terms?
5. Why does the Bible equate idolatry with adultery?
6. What does God want more than anything else?

Chapter 15
A New Identity

On April 20, 1999, two young men began an attack they had long been planning on their high school. Within hours, fifteen people lay dead, including the perpetrators. Another twenty-four suffered injuries, some serious, most by gunfire. Not only was the Columbine mass shooting a tragic event, it also unleashed a wave of evil across the United States, with other "copycat" shootings and immeasurable pain to follow.

While mass events garner widespread attention, more localized news reports address shootings and other types of violence day in and day out. Much of the attention has focused on guns, but a scarlet thread runs through it all: the quest for a significant identity.

Research has shown that approximately 98% of mass shooters have been male.[1] And though mental illness has been a contributing factor, the vast majority have struggled with *identity* issues because of family dynamics, bullying, and social rejection—or the fear thereof. In a convoluted way, taking the life of another is seen as an opportunity to make a name for oneself—or at least to avoid public humiliation.

OUR QUEST FOR GLORY

Mass violence grabs our attention, but such acts form the proverbial tip of the iceberg. The quest for a meaningful identity has always been a key driver to the human condition, becoming more of a factor as fatherlessness increases and the stability of family life erodes. In a quest for glory and significance, people will cling to unhealthy relationships, consume their vitality with work, and trample potential competitors as they stand on their toes reaching for status and wealth.

---

1. Kim Mills, American Psychological Association, "209: How to Stop Mass Shootings, with Jillian Peterson, PhD," October 2022, in *Speaking of Psychology*, produced by American Psychological Association, podcast audio, 34:30, accessed February 18, 2025, https://www.apa.org/news/podcasts/speaking-of-psychology/mass-shootings.

Ironic. I cannot find a better word to adequately describe our identity struggles. Looking back at the first chapter of Genesis we read:

> Then God said, "Let Us make man in Our image, according to Our likeness; and let them rule over the fish of the sea and over the birds of the sky and over the cattle and over all the earth, and over every creeping thing that creeps on the earth." God created man in His own image, in the image of God He created him; male and female He created them. Genesis 1:26–27

Can we think of a greater honor than being created in the image of the One who brought all things into existence? None of the animals were created in God's image. No trees or streams or mountains were created in God's image. Not even the angels in heaven were created in God's image. *Only humans* were created in the image of the Almighty. The Lord has gifted us with honor above all creatures, and yet we are plagued by identity issues.

God is glorious in every way, and He created us to be "clothed" with that glory. But as a consequence of disobedience, we have been spiritually stripped bare and left naked. Still, the innate desire lingers. How we long to return to the former glory which humanity squandered! And herein lies the problem with pride: it seeks to find significance *apart from* God. Using means such as appearance, performance, possessions, knowledge, status, and our association with others, we spend our energies in hot pursuit of glory. But our efforts never fully satisfy, and so we must renew them with the rising sun of each morning dawn.

SOCIAL STRATIFICATION

Our quest for glory produces *social stratification* through which we judge people based on their abilities to measure up to an array of social standards. This stratification, in turn, creates conflict as the elite proclaim their greatness while often belittling—and oppressing—those they view as inferior. Offended by the denial of their own quests for significance, the less fortunate then seethe with bitterness and hatred, sometimes leading to violence.

A New Identity

We dare never forget the *Big Lie* that characterized the *Great Temptation* in the garden of Eden: "You will be like God" (Genesis 3:5). With profound insight, the supposedly mythical story found in the supposedly antiquated Bible identifies a primary source of our human brokenness: an impossible quest for an unattainable identity. According to the Scriptures, this quest to be like God apart from God opened the door for conflict, suffering, destruction, and death in our once-pristine world. How many of today's mental health issues and social struggles are the continued fallout from that ill-fated pursuit?

Lest we sink into morbid discouragement, let us not forget the creation/fall/redemption pattern that characterizes the Bible. And nowhere does this pattern apply more than with our longing for a meaningful identity. We were created for glory in God's image. We forfeited that glory, becoming subject to a plaguing deficiency. And we can know glory restored by becoming esteemed children of God. This is no minor issue in the dynamics of emotional well-being.

Jesus stepped from the height of heaven's throne to embrace the shame of a Roman cross so we might be restored to His glorious image. *The good news of the kingdom of God is not just a message of tomorrow's destiny, but also of today's identity.*

> He came to His own, and those who were His own did not receive Him. But as many as received Him, to them He gave the right to become children of God, even to those who believe in His name, who were born, not of blood nor of the will of the flesh nor of the will of man, but of God. John 1:11–13

Talk about good news! Do we realize the implications? Can we think of a greater honor than becoming a beloved child of the King of kings and Lord of lords? If we have such favor with the God who created our vast universe, what else do we need? He will take care of everything in His time.

ESTEEMED BY HEAVEN

I am both inspired and challenged by the apostle Paul's letter to the Ephesian church:

> And you were dead in your trespasses and sins, in which you formerly walked according to the course of this world, according to the prince of the power of the air, of the spirit that is now working in the sons of disobedience. Among them we too all formerly lived in the lusts of our flesh, indulging the desires of the flesh and of the mind, and were by nature children of wrath, even as the rest. But God, being rich in mercy, because of His great love with which He loved us, even when we were dead in our transgressions, made us alive together with Christ (by grace you have been saved), and raised us up with Him, and seated us with Him in the heavenly places in Christ Jesus, so that in the ages to come He might show the surpassing riches of His grace in kindness toward us in Christ Jesus. Ephesians 2:1–7

Who among us is worthy of heaven's favor? We have already learned how far short we fall. But God had other plans!

Being seated with Christ in the heavenly places has much to do with our royal status in the eyes of heaven. Picture, for a minute, the banquet table of a magnificent king. Who do you see sitting at the table? Visiting dignitaries? Elite government officials? How about the king's own children? They find lofty status in *their father's* greatness.

People labor hard to establish a sense of significance by seeking to measure up to social standards of all kinds. Either haughtiness or despair result, depending upon the success of their efforts. This has been our human way throughout history.

But with the kingdom of God, a person's identity comes as a *gift of grace* through the sacrificial work of Christ; it is not something we can ever earn. And so it is that our service to God and humanity is the *outflow* of a significance *already* established. We do not labor *for* validation but *from* validation. The difference in our lives is seismic—like that between life and death.

What does it matter what mortals think? We can find no greater identity than being called "a child of God" by the King of Glory. Every other pursuit of significance amounts to chasing after the wind. Are you chasing the wind?

Digging Deeper Into Chapter Fifteen

Father. What an emotion-laden word, meaning many things for many people! For a long time, pain would have been my response. My father was in his late fifties when I was born, becoming sickly and reclusive during my early elementary years. He passed on when I was a teen, and though he lived in our home until then, I felt very much abandoned. *Numb* is probably the best word to describe my response when he died. I cannot begin to explain how my father's emotional absence contributed to my insecurities and all-around struggle with life.

I have met others along my life journey who experienced even greater pain from fathers who were verbally or physically abusive. The very person who should have provided love, security, and protection had instead violated a sacred trust. Thankfully, not all fatherhood stories are bad. My wife had a great relationship with her dad and was deeply grieved when he passed from this world.

By nature, we are inclined to project the images of our earthly fathers on God the Father in heaven. In some cases, a good experience helps to create a healthy perspective of the Lord, but others can be grossly distorted. And the reality is that no human father can compare to the Author of life and love.

Several other factors complicate our perspective of God. The old covenant of law can taint our vision to see Him as cruel and vindictive, when, in reality, it should point us toward His grace. Western culture has also clouded our vision. Media commonly portrays fathers as bumbling, negligent, or cruel. And the backlash against the oppressive "patriarchy" of some cultures has painted a broad brush to discolor anything related to fatherhood.

Why does any of this matter? Whether we want to admit it or not, our fathers help shape our identity. And though we all struggle with an unhealthy pursuit of glory and significance, those problems are compounded by bad, unhealthy, or nonexistent relationships with our earthly fathers. This is one area in life where the eyes of our hearts need to be opened to see our heavenly Father through an accurate lens.

See also: Ephesians 3:14–21

While some people struggle with the concept of family because of bad personal experiences, the ideal is in itself beautiful. And though sinful humanity has at times corrupted the design, God the Father is the source of what is meant to be an environment characterized by *unconditional love*.

I have also learned that God is a father to the fatherless. And though I longed for a close relationship with my biological father, I have experienced the eternal truth that the Lord provides a special blessing of grace to those lacking that healthy connection. I have also learned that even when my heavenly Father appears to be absent, He is actively working all things to my good.

Dig deeper: Psalms 68:5–6
Romans 8:26–39

I find great meaning in knowing that the gospel is an identity message. The good news is not just about where we go after we die, but also who we become through the new covenant. To be a chosen and beloved child of God—I do not entirely understand it, but nothing compares!

Dig deeper: John 1:9–18

QUESTIONS

1. What does it mean to be created in the image of God?
2. What is ironic about the temptation to be like God?
3. How do you see the quest for a meaningful identity playing out in the world around you?
4. Why does identity matter so much to us?
5. In what way is the gospel an identity message?
6. With one or two words, describe your view of God the Father.

Chapter 16
Free!

Can you recall the worst terror you have ever felt? How about the deepest feeling of anxiety? Depression? Dread? Grief? Abandonment? Loneliness? If you add them together and multiply the cumulative despair by several billion, you might get a taste of how the Son of God felt in the garden of Gethsemane as He prayed to the heavenly Father. And that was only a foretaste of the agony Jesus would experience as the sins of humanity were heaped upon His willing shoulders.

As humans, we are prone to seeking our own way, but Jesus made a complete surrender to the heavenly Father when it would cost Him the most. Our Savior's choice in Gethsemane represents the greatest victory of the will that has ever been achieved on earth.

> And He was saying, "Abba! Father! All things are possible for You; remove this cup from Me; yet not what I will, but what You will." Mark 14:36

As Christ's shameful and torturous death on a wooden cross drew nearer, the full realization of His choice began to dawn and a trembling sense of dread flooded His heart. With the potential options racing through His mind, Jesus understood there to be no other way. But He did have another choice. The Son of God could have forgone the cross and returned to heaven as the still-glorious King of kings and Lord of lords. But every human ever born would have perished under the weight of sin, death, and judgment. And that our Savior could not bear. Love—real, sacrificial and caring love—left Him with no other choice but to yield to the Father's will.

We can be sure that if another option existed for us to avoid the pain of judgment and experience the glories of heaven, Jesus would have kept His distance from the cross. But why was there no other way? To better understand, we must comprehend God's intent.

FREEDOM

What was the heavenly Father's primary goal in sending His Son to the cross? What was He seeking to accomplish? What great purpose could be worth such extreme pain and suffering? The plan was for Jesus to restore the relationship between God and humanity. But not just restore it; the Son of God established a new kind of covenant for a new kind of relationship between the Creator and His prized creations. God would be intimate with humans in a love relationship like never before known. That relationship, however, required a vital element of life first seen in the garden paradise of Eden: *freedom*.

I cannot imagine most people viewing the words "freedom" and "Christianity" as complementary. They think the Bible is about rules, restrictions, and required religious rituals. Freedom does not seem to fit the pattern. But freedom is necessary if love is to be a two-way street.

God could force us to do His will, or simply rewire us so we would know only obedience. But then it would not be love. Who wants an intimate relationship with a robot? Jesus pioneered a fresh path to God—the only one possible for us to be both *free and near.*

Not only are we cleansed of our sins by the blood of Jesus, He also clothes us in His "robe" of righteous perfection. Scholars call this "imputed" righteousness. Amazingly, when God looks upon His children, He chooses to see the righteous perfection of Jesus and not the many shortcomings and flaws that plague our lives.

> He made Him who knew no sin to be sin on our behalf, so that we might become the righteousness of God in Him. 2 Corinthians 5:21

Such a statement stops me in my tracks! That Christ would become sin so I might be esteemed with heavenly favor seems too good to be true. It is not a concept I would have ever envisioned apart from the Bible.

When I was in high school, athletes could get varsity jackets. And those who performed well enough would earn a class letter to be displayed prominently on their left chest. Numerous pins could be earned and added to proclaim the student's athletic prowess.

Early on, varsity jackets were primarily a male thing, but females could still wear them as badges of honor. If a young woman was lucky enough to date the high school quarterback, for example, he would likely drape his varsity jacket over her shoulders. So it was that everyone would immediately recognize her favor with the seemingly most important guy in that graduating class.

We sometimes struggle to grasp the concept of imputed righteousness because, as far as we can tell, we are still us. We still have our ups and downs, our struggles and failures. And yet, God chooses to see us as though we are wearing the "varsity jacket" only Jesus could have earned. Then, He sets about transforming our lives through a process called "sanctification" so we actually become more like Jesus.

"This all sounds wonderful, but what does it have to do with freedom?" you might ask. Think back to the events of Eden with me. Why did the serpent tempt Adam and Eve to eat from the forbidden tree? Was he trying to usher them into newfound freedom through which they could joyfully follow their hearts' desires? Never! Evil always seeks to blind and bind. Unfettered control was his goal, and sin his useful servant.

God reigns, but He does not control. And the two differ greatly. Evil seeks to control. But our Creator already possesses all power and authority. Freedom never frightens real power.

The promise of fulfillment through unrestrained actions is merely a guise by dark forces to ensnare us. With the right hand sin entices us through the allure of freedom and fulfillment, and with the left it silently shackles our wrists. But sin's power to enslave goes far beyond mere desire.

THE LAW OF LIBERTY

True freedom has nothing to do with an individualistic, self-seeking, and lawless mindset in which just about any kind of behavior is acceptable. It is a collective, social freedom that sprouts from internal victory over selfish desires. If we consider democracy, for example, it works by a system of laws that respect the rights of all individuals. But only as a nation's citizens submit themselves to laws designed for the greater good can a democracy thrive, or even survive. And regardless of the laws involved, such a government cannot survive long when its people worship at the altar of self.

The kingdom of God has its laws, but they are not burdensome. Kingdom laws do not try to control behavior and address every potential problem that might arise. Nor does God impress upon us the constant need to obey rules so we can be good and righteous people who are acceptable in His sight.

The Great Temptation unfolded under the tree of the knowledge of good and evil. This means the devil enslaved humanity by enticing Adam and Eve to enter a world of seeking goodness and righteousness by measuring up to standards of perfection. It is this constant reaching for the stars that leads us into bondage. Those who believe the Christian life is characterized by obeying rules and measuring up to standards will be bound by pride and selfish desire.

The primary law of God's kingdom is simple, yet not simplistic. The Bible refers to it as the "law of liberty" (James 1:25). Also known as the "royal law," or the "law of the King," the *law of love* encapsulates all. According to Jesus, the command to love God with all one's heart, soul, and mind, along with the command to love others, sums up *all* the teachings of the old covenant law and *all* the proclamations of the prophets (Matthew 22:34-40). Even the Ten Commandments are fulfilled by the law of love (Romans 13:8-10). Paul also wrote:

> For the love of Christ controls us, having concluded this, that one died for all, therefore all died; and He died for all, so that they who live might no longer live for themselves, but for Him who died and rose again on their behalf. 2 Corinthians 5:14-15

We now come full circle to where we began this chapter, with love being the compelling force behind our actions. No long lists of rules. Only pure desire for goodness, wholeness, and meaning.

A country in which the citizens are free to do as they want, but choose to be motivated by love? This is paradise and the good news of the kingdom!

Digging Deeper
Into Chapter Sixteen

Have you ever seriously contemplated humanity's fall from paradise and the painful consequences it caused? The serpent used fewer than *fifty* words to entice Adam and Eve to disobey their Creator and join his rebellion. How did he do it? By distorting the reality of God.

Dig deeper: Genesis 3:1-7

Some people speak in terms of "my truth" and "your truth," but God's truth supersedes them all. In other terms, God's reality is what matters most. That reality includes seeing our Creator accurately, discerning our true state, and understanding how He sees us. All the while, the devil and his lackeys strive to keep us deceived and in the dark.

According to Jesus Himself, a primary reason He stepped down from the glory of heaven was to testify on earth to the truth.

Dig deeper: John 18:28-38

Jesus came to our planet to reveal the reality of God. And it is within this reality that we find freedom.

Dig deeper: John 8:31-47

When Adam and Eve took and ate the forbidden fruit, their eyes were opened, and they became aware of standards of perfection which enslaved them. At the same time, their eyes were closed to an accurate understanding of God and His ways. And so it is that darkness covered our world until the arrival of Christ.

Becoming a Christian involves turning to the light so God can open our eyes to His reality. For this to happen, we must honor and pursue truth apart from personal agendas. You see, this is where so many of humanity's problems find their roots: in our unwillingness to let go of what we want reality to be.

Spiritual truth is the antidote for the deception that keeps us bound in sin, but we must first recognize our need and be willing to embrace God's reality. Is this not where our problems lie? Selfishness, pride, and insecurity all tempt us to stubbornly close our eyes and ears to truth. A person bound by addiction, for example, cannot break free without facing the reality of his or her situation.

The Greek orator Demosthenes once said, "Nothing is easier than self-deceit. For what every man wishes, that he also believes to be true." And Julius Caesar reportedly stated, "Men in general are quick to believe that which they wish to be true." Both statements provide a timeless and accurate representation of our human tendencies.

"He who has ears to hear, let him hear," was a phrase spoken by Jesus on multiple occasions (Matthew 11:15; Mark 4:23; Revelation 2:7). The Son of Man knew His teachings were challenging and difficult to accept. And yet He never backed down from proclaiming the truth because He always had the best interests of humanity in mind.

It seems we are left with an uncomfortable choice. We either lay aside our emotions and desires to accept truths against our liking, or we stubbornly hold to our own way and remain bound by the powers of sin and darkness. I do not always like truth, but I love the freeing effect it has on my life!

See also: Proverbs 1:20–33

QUESTIONS

1. What made Jesus' choice to yield to the Father's will in the garden of Gethsemane so significant?
2. How have you traditionally viewed the relationship between freedom and Christianity?
3. Why is our freedom of vital importance to God?
4. What is the law of liberty?
5. Why is it vital for us to see God as He truly is?
6. What are some barriers to truth that have kept you bound?

Chapter 17
The Gift of the Holy Spirit

I would welcome an in-person conversation with Jesus. Sitting down. Face to face. Inhaling the aroma of a fresh coffee, I would ask Him to expound upon dinosaurs and the age of the universe and women in ministry. I would want to know why some people are healed and some are not, and the deeper meaning of His statements regarding money. I would pepper Him with questions about sexuality and divorce, and if the conversation went as hoped, I might even begin to query about eternal judgment and the unreached pygmies in Africa.

If I could have a conversation with Jesus, I would not want it to end. My well of questions might run quickly dry, but I would continue to ask, just to hear Him talk. Sitting at the Lord's feet for hours on end would be just fine with me.

But if I could have a never-ending in-person conversation with Jesus, you could not—not unless you were part of a very small and select group. Limitations of time and space would allow only a few people to sit in His physical presence. And that is why Jesus no longer walks this earth in human flesh.

PENTECOST

Acts 1:9–11 tells the story of Jesus ascending to heaven right before His disciples' eyes. Dumbfounded, they hardly knew what to do. But it did not take them long to figure it out—especially after the *Day of Pentecost.*

Pentecost was a Jewish holiday celebrated fifty days after the Passover lambs were sacrificed to cover their sins. It was on that day, fifty sunrises after Christ's crucifixion, that the *Holy Spirit* came upon God's people in an unlikely way as they gathered for prayer.

> When the day of Pentecost had come, they were all together in one place. And suddenly there came from heaven a noise like a violent rushing wind, and it filled the whole house where they were sitting. And there appeared to them tongues as of fire distributing themselves, and they rested on each one of them. And they were all filled with the Holy Spirit and began to speak with other tongues, as the Spirit was giving them utterance.
>
> Now there were Jews living in Jerusalem, devout men from every nation under heaven. And when this sound occurred, the crowd came together, and were bewildered because each one of them was hearing them speak in his own language. They were amazed and astonished, saying, "Why, are not all these who are speaking Galileans? And how is it that we each hear them in our own language to which we were born? Parthians and Medes and Elamites, and residents of Mesopotamia, Judea and Cappadocia, Pontus and Asia, Phrygia and Pamphylia, Egypt and the districts of Libya around Cyrene, and visitors from Rome, both Jews and proselytes, Cretans and Arabs—we hear them in our own tongues speaking of the mighty deeds of God." And they all continued in amazement and great perplexity, saying to one another, "What does this mean?" But others were mocking and saying, "They are full of sweet wine." Acts 2:1–13

Great perplexity? I would say so! Jesus, in human form, was limited by time and space. So when He told the disciples it was to their advantage for Him to go away (John 16:7), He had something greater in mind. In the context of that passage, the Son of God had been speaking of the *Holy Spirit*.

This strange event marked the birth of the Christian church. We can have all kinds of definitions and descriptions, but from a Biblical perspective, it is the Holy Spirit who makes the church the church.

THE HOLY SPIRIT

Some Christians hesitate to speak about the Holy Spirit because they view Him like a distant relative who nobody quite knows what to do

The Gift of the Holy Spirit

with. Others bristle when there is talk of the Spirit's work because He can be as unpredictable in our day as Jesus was in His. And, of course, there are people who do things in the name of the Spirit that the Spirit Himself would never consider.

As a necessary starting point, we understand the Holy Spirit to be a "He" and not an "it." We are not talking about an impersonal force that can be manipulated for good or evil, but the third Person of the Trinity—indeed, God Himself.

Practically speaking, the Holy Spirit is the heavenly "agent" who accomplishes the purposes of God on earth. The Spirit is everywhere; there is nowhere He is not. And His "job description" is almost as long as the Bible itself.

Perhaps most significant to us is His *nearness*. And even more than His nearness, His *indwelling*. When a person becomes a Christian by yielding to Jesus as King, His sacred blood cleanses the stench and stain of sin. This allows the Holy Spirit to enter the person's heart and set up a homestead. God's presence does not dwell in religious temples or church buildings, but within His people (1 Corinthians 3:16-17; 1 Corinthians 6:19). We are not gods ourselves, but *vessels of honor* in which the Almighty God lives (2 Timothy 2:20-21).

The Holy Spirit is near—and not just in religious settings. He will dwell within us, be with us, and go with us wherever we go. While in the car, waiting in line at a grocery store, even while cleaning the house, we can commune with our Creator.

Through the Spirit, we are blessed to commune with God in the most intimate way possible. Emotions are readily understood and prayers instantly heard. He comforts and encourages us during times of hardship and loss, enabling us to experience heaven's peace in the least likely times. The very thought is mind-altering!

Sometimes the Spirit "convicts" us of sin or ill-advised actions. We might bristle because His conviction often runs contrary to the grain of human will, but it is always for our best. With an eye for a blessed future, the Spirit convicts us of sin so our relationship with God can remain unhindered and to protect us from painful regrets.

The Holy Spirit does *not* condemn us or flood our minds with guilt. It is the devil who accuses and condemns, and surprisingly, so does our own conscience. Being driven by law-based standards, the conscience finds its roots in the tree of the knowledge of good and evil.

EMPOWERED!

A primary work of the Holy Spirit involves *empowerment*. In ways that stretch the imagination, He enables us to do things not humanly possible. This involves living in dominion over the power of sin and serving others through spiritual gifts beyond our natural abilities.

I struggle to understand how the Christian faith would work apart from the presence and power of the Holy Spirit. We are not talking about a humanistic endeavor driven by natural logic and characterized by innate intelligence. We are called to daily dwell in the presence of the eternal God who enlightens and empowers us. It is the same Spirit, the Bible tells us, that raised Christ from the dead (Romans 8:11).

Jesus also said the Holy Spirit can be compared to a *blowing wind* which we cannot fully understand (John 3:8). I suppose that is what makes the Spirit's presence both scary and exhilarating. But we must always remember that we are talking about God Himself. Because of Christ's shed blood, His nearness is always to our benefit.

Though every believer is indwelt by the Holy Spirit, we do not always live in His fullness. It is possible to "quench the Spirit" (1 Thessalonians 5:19), which is often the result of willful sin—especially treating other Christians with contempt. Instead, we should seek to be filled and empowered by His presence (Ephesians 5:18).

We face obvious challenges because the Holy Spirit is not of human flesh. We cannot sit and talk with Him the way the disciples talked with Jesus. Still, He is more than adept at accomplishing His purposes in our lives.

Part of the Spirit's empowerment involves what we might call "wisdom gifts." He provides both *revelation* and *illumination* of eternal truth, enables us to *discern* what is happening around us, and imparts *wisdom* for skillful living. And as we yield to His will, the Holy Spirit *guides* us to fulfill the plans and purposes of God.

The bigger concern involves our willingness to believe and yield to His will. His mysterious presence might challenge me at times, but I cannot begin to imagine life without Him!

Digging Deeper Into Chapter Seventeen

More likely than not, you have experienced the pain of a broken promise. Such violations of trust hurt, deeply, and for a very long time—especially when promises are repeatedly broken by someone we should be able to depend upon. Over time, we might find ourselves struggling to trust anyone, including God. But to equate our perfect Creator with self-centered humans is a seismic error.

Not only is God in the habit of making promises, He is in the habit of keeping the promises He makes. No exceptions. If we think circumstances speak otherwise, our understanding is lacking. As much as people in the modern West struggle with the concept of absolutes, the Almighty is *absolutely faithful* to His promises.

To illustrate, God promised that a descendant of King David would rule Israel forever. But the nation went astray, and its succession of kings came to a tragic end through exile in Babylon. Faithful Jews struggled with the apparent contradiction between God's promises and their reality.

Dig deeper: Psalm 89:19–45

We know now that Jesus was the eternal King promised by God, and in retrospect, His plan makes perfect sense. But in their day, painful circumstances appeared to proclaim a different story.

Another long-standing promise of God involves the gift of the Holy Spirit. In old covenant times, the Spirit of God would sometimes come temporarily upon select individuals for specific purposes (1 Samuel 10:1–13). With a few of the prophets such as Elijah and Elisha, the Spirit's anointing seemed to be more permanent, although God made no guarantees. And when David committed a heinous sin by sleeping with Bathsheba and having her husband murdered, the king rightly feared the Holy Spirit might leave him (Psalm 51:10–11).

Much about the old covenant was temporary, but it was all intended to lead toward our eternal new covenant in Christ. Through the prophet Joel, God promised a powerful outpouring of the Holy Spirit.

Dig deeper: Joel 2:28-29

According to the apostle Peter, this promise found its fulfillment on the Day of Pentecost (Acts 2:16-18). But that was only the beginning!

> Peter said to them, "Repent, and each of you be baptized in the name of Jesus Christ for the forgiveness of your sins; and you will receive the gift of the Holy Spirit. For the promise is for you and your children and for all who are far off, as many as the Lord our God will call to Himself." Acts 2:38-39

Today, we are living in the fulfillment of God's promise. And what can be greater than having God Himself dwell within us? Can a more intimate relationship be possible? Never! And with the Creator of our cosmos dwelling in our hearts, the possibilities are limitless.

See also: John 14:8-19

So, where do we begin? We rejoice and rest secure, celebrating the promise of His presence made possible through the blood of Jesus. As we seek to know Him and align with His ways, everything else will follow in its time.

QUESTIONS

1. What makes God's presence the best promise ever?
2. What role does the Holy Spirit serve in the church?
3. What does it mean to be "convicted" by the Holy Spirit?
4. In what ways can the Holy Spirit be compared to a blowing wind?
5. Why should we seek to be filled with the Holy Spirit?
6. What limitations are you placing upon the Holy Spirit's work in your life?

Chapter 18

Communion

I have experienced some extreme highs and lows throughout the course of my life. I suppose that is common to all humanity. Even so, I cannot imagine the depths of emotion Jesus must have felt in His final hours before the cross.

The Son of God had stepped from the throne of heaven to live in obscurity on earth. Then, for over three years, the self-proclaimed "Son of Man" poured His life into a small group of disciples. While ministering healing, freedom, and provision to large crowds, Jesus saw up close and personal the needs of humanity. Of course, the selfish, self-exalting ways of those in authority were never far from view because their actions influenced just about every arena of life. Now, here He was, about to leave it all to return to His Father in heaven, but only after suffering a torturous, shameful death for the sins of humanity. With deep emotion, the Son of God established the *new covenant*:

> When the hour had come, He reclined at the table, and the apostles with Him. And He said to them, "I have earnestly desired to eat this Passover with you before I suffer; for I say to you, I shall never again eat it until it is fulfilled in the kingdom of God." And when He had taken a cup and given thanks, He said, "Take this and share it among yourselves; for I say to you, I will not drink of the fruit of the vine from now on until the kingdom of God comes." And when He had taken some bread and given thanks, He broke it and gave it to them, saying, "This is My body which is given for you; do this in remembrance of Me." And in the same way He took the cup after they had eaten, saying, "This cup which is poured out for you is the new covenant in My blood." Luke 22:14–20

COVENANTAL BONDS

Jesus' last meal on earth (a.k.a. the "Last Supper") symbolized the purpose of His sacrificial death, revealed the driving desire of His heart, and established a new relationship with God, unlike anything ever imagined by humanity. To this day, one of the defining elements of Christian practice involves the taking of *communion*—also referred to as the "Eucharist" by some. And while the practice is nearly universal amongst professing Christians, one of the core elements—*covenant*—mostly eludes our grasp.

A covenant is a type of agreement, similar to a contract, but of a higher order. Ancient covenants—sometimes called "treaties"—were often established between powerful rulers and their subjects to end hostilities. But other covenants were intended to be more *relational* as participants sought to create a *legal kinship*. Such continues to be the case with the *marriage covenant*. When two unrelated people enter a marriage covenant, they form a new family entity—a "kinship tribe," so to speak. And if they were to adopt an orphan, that child would become a legal part of the family with all the associated rights.

Sometimes, creating a family bond might be transactional to garner money or political power. But family bonds are mostly driven by a desire to be together. A man and a woman marry because they want to share their lives. Moreover, the expense of adopting a child is driven by a deep desire to enfold the little one into their household.

The examples of marriage and adoption help provide a glimpse of Christ's passion to share a last meal with His disciples. A similar desire steeled His resolve in the face of a torturous cross, knowing full well what His sacrificial death would accomplish. *The Lord's heart ever beats for His children to be near to Him and to one another.*

Sadly, our world's perspective of family often falls short. I will sometimes watch a television show and come away asking, "Is that it? Is that the best they have to offer?" This is especially true regarding the concept of family. After one character experiences a significant loss, another asks if she can call upon any family members for help. The response typically declares that the person's coworkers are her family—that is, as long as the writers continue to keep her in the script.

The concept of family transcends fluctuating human desires through its lasting covenantal bonds. I understand the ideal often eludes us, but these bonds can also carry us through seasons when our feelings might waver. Debi and I have been married for over forty years. We have experienced times good and bad, but our covenant connection has helped us navigate the challenges we have faced. The resulting stability has also created favorable environments for the growth and development of our children and grandchildren.

WHAT MATTERS MOST

Through the new covenant in His blood, Jesus established a new and even higher order of family. As beloved members of God's household, we can have fellowship with Him and with one another (our focus in the next chapter). And, as we tend to learn over time, when it comes to family, it is our relationships that matter most.

But just as we can lose sight of what is truly important regarding our relationships, so too might religious practices miss their intended mark. Acts 17:22-34 records a fascinating discussion between the apostle Paul and a group of philosophical Greeks, who, according to Paul, worshiped in ignorance.

> "The God who made the world and all things in it, since He is Lord of heaven and earth, does not dwell in temples made with hands; nor is He served by human hands, as though He needed anything, since He Himself gives to all people life and breath and all things; and He made from one man every nation of mankind to live on all the face of the earth, having determined their appointed times and the boundaries of their habitation, that they would seek God, if perhaps they might grope for Him and find Him, though He is not far from each one of us; for in Him we live and move and exist, as even some of your own poets have said, 'For we also are His children.'" Acts 17:24-28

That God can be near and yet far both fascinates and troubles me. In a very general sense of the word, the Lord is always near. Being omnipresent, our Creator exists everywhere at the same time. But the recognition of His manifest presence reveals a different perspective. God can be near, but not close. In other words, His invisible Spirit might surround me while I remain "distant" and clueless of His ways. Is this not the great, impossible problem of humanity? God is always near, but we remain blind to His presence, driven by polluted and errant perceptions of heaven's King.

Jesus established the essence of religious practice in His *High Priestly Prayer* after the Last Supper: "This is eternal life, that they may know You, the only true God, and Jesus Christ whom You have sent" (John 17:3). And this enviable opportunity becomes ours through the new covenant in Christ's blood. For this reason, I like to refer to the communion cup as the "cup of nearness." Through communion, we remember all He has done for us, along with His constant nearness.

Knowing the Lord and His nearness does not happen by default, but through an intentional process initiated by our Creator and responded to by us. God never intended communion to be about ritual, but about *connection*. Do you know what the heavenly Father wants? He wants us to connect with Him and with other members of His family to the best degree possible for broken, imperfect, and sometimes sinful Christians.

His eye does not focus on how well we carry out religious rituals. The God of heaven and earth wants us to *abide* in Him (John 15:1–17). Living by faith through the royal law of love, we can *dwell* in the Lord's presence and experience a multitude of profound blessings.

To live close to God is to be changed as the *fruit of the Holy Spirit* grows in our hearts. Love, joy, peace, patience, kindness, goodness, faithfulness, gentleness, and self-control—these virtues characterize us more and more as we dwell in the Spirit's presence (Galatians 5:22–23).

God is glorified as the fruit of His Spirit flourishes within us. The process might not be linear, and there will be times when we feel as though we are making little progress, but that is all part of the growing process. My greater concern is for those who follow rules and obey rituals, but whose hearts are never changed.

Through Jesus, heaven has taken the most extreme initiative possible. May we not squander this amazing opportunity to dwell in the presence of the Almighty!

Digging Deeper
Into Chapter Eighteen

Each nation has its own set of cultural customs, and that also holds true for many activities and professions. But sometimes, a culture does not make sense to outsiders. An actor, for example, might encourage a fellow actor to "break a leg" as an encouragement for good luck, but to someone unfamiliar with the profession, an attempt at encouragement might sound like an insult.

There can be multiple reasons why Christianity might not make sense to a person. To begin, we view life through a temporal, natural lens, while God's perspective is spiritual and eternal. And so it is that our Creator thinks on a different plane than humanity.

Dig deeper: Isaiah 55:6-13

The Bible also contains language that differs from ours. For example, *sanctification* is not a word you will likely hear outside of Christian circles. And then there are cultural differences. Some might be tied to cultural customs of ancient times—such as blood sacrifices. These and other differences remind us of the importance of seeking wisdom from God and dedicating ourselves to learning the dynamics of our faith.

See also: Genesis 15

Christianity does not make sense to some people because it is embodied by the *covenant culture* in which the Bible was penned. Modern minds—especially those in the Western World—tend not to think in covenantal terms. Worse still, we often take offense at the ideals of Scripture because we do not grasp the covenantal context in which they were formed. Allow me to highlight four primary issues.

First, people often struggle with significant doubts about God's goodness because of the harsh judgments meted out during Old Testament times—especially after the Mosaic law was given. They fail to grasp the law-based nature of the old covenant. Humanity chose law when Adam and Eve ate from the tree of the knowledge of good and evil, and God gave the Mosaic law as an extension of that choice to teach us the futility of our ways. The old covenant was a much-needed stepping stone to lead us to the new and better covenant in Christ; it was never intended to provide an accurate reflection of God's mindset.

Dig deeper: Hebrews 8:7–13

Second, we can make similar statements regarding spiritual curses and eternal judgment. Humanity brought curses on itself because we violated a sacred trust. And the punishment of hell was originally prepared for the devil and his angels (Matthew 25:41). Had humans not joined Lucifer's rebellion by eating from the forbidden tree, hell would have been a non-issue.

Our third issue regards marriage and sexuality. Sex outside of the marriage covenant is regarded as sinful and immoral because it violates a sacred covenant established by our Creator for humanity's good. Accordingly, love is more a covenantal concept than a vague ideal.

Dig deeper: Genesis 2:18–25

Finally, we recognize the sacredness of covenantal relationships because of the sacred nature of trust. A healthy life is built upon healthy relationships, but real intimacy is impossible apart from trust.

The teachings of the Bible begin to form a beautiful portrait as we understand the covenantal nature of our faith.

QUESTIONS

1. What makes it difficult to understand Christianity apart from a covenantal mindset?
2. What does the new covenant mean to you?
3. How is communion related to the new covenant?
4. How does covenant relate to God's design for the family?
5. How does covenant relate to God's design for the church?
6. What makes covenants sacred?

Chapter 19

Why So Many Denominations?

Aside from the physical parts, one specific difference separates my wife and me as much as any. When riding in the passenger seat of our car during a trip, Debi will gather various bags at her feet. This puts her e-reader and other "necessities" within easy reach. For my part, I cannot stand having anything at my feet. Without room to move and recline, I feel near claustrophobic. The difference might come from the years of having toddlers clinging to her legs because it seems to represent a common marker between males and females.

Debi and I have other differences, of course. I like pickled beets; she cannot stand them. And while I enjoy the entire blend of my homemade trail mix, she picks out and eats the more expensive ingredients. I would be happy with temperatures in the mid-seventies all year; she prefers warmer air. And so it is that my plan to move to the equator and live high on a mountainside has never come to fruition. My wife will go canoeing with me, but only in the middle of the day when fishing is worst. I enjoy a good hymn every now and again, but Debi grew up in a small church with bad singing and poor instrument playing. Hymns tend not to warm her heart. I could expound upon many more differences between us, but I think you get the point.

We humans are much the same, but we are also diverse. We have different tastes, abilities, and preferences in music. And because of our many differences, it should come as no surprise that we have many churches and denominations.

A certain amount of diversity is to be expected among Jesus' followers, but in all honesty, I feel embarrassed by some of the attitudes and actions I encounter in various Christian circles. Sometimes, I will even mutter sarcastically, "If that's what being a Christian is like, I don't think I want to be one."

I cannot say I have ever seriously contemplated walking away from the Lord, but I have had to work through some daunting struggles regarding our collective representation of Christ. Rather than leave, I have decided to contend for change from within. That is why I write books and serve in ministry. With all God has provided for us, we can do better. And with all that is at stake, we must do better.

No small number of people profess to follow Christ while failing to take the Christian Scriptures seriously, and so we are compelled to draw doctrinal lines. I do not see how we can call ourselves "Christians" if we do not honor the teachings of Jesus and His apostles.

CORE DOCTRINES

The Bible illuminates *core doctrines* that bind Christians together. Other issues might be important, but they are not as essential as the core elements. With many of our beliefs, we have freedom to differ. But regarding the central tenets of our faith, there can be no compromise. I do not consider myself the ultimate authority for spiritual truth, but the following five items represent sound Biblical doctrine:

- **The Bible** - the Bible is the only inspired, infallible, and authoritative writing related to spiritual matters (2 Timothy 3:16–17).

- **The Trinity** - Father, Son, and Holy Spirit form the "Godhead" as Three-In-one (2 Corinthians 13:14).

- **Jesus** - Born to a virgin, Jesus was both fully God and fully man. Guilty of no offense against heaven, He willingly died a torturous death on a Roman cross as a sacrifice for human sin. Jesus then rose from the grave because death could not hold Him (Acts 2:24; 1 Corinthians 15:3–5).

- **Salvation** - All people have been born into sin, which causes all to sin willfully. We cannot redeem ourselves or earn favor with God, and so our salvation comes only by grace through faith as we are cleansed by the sacrificial blood of Christ. This truth is the foundation upon which the New Testament and the good news of the gospel rest (Acts 4:12; Ephesians 2:8–9).

- **Marriage** - Marriage involves a *sacred covenant* between one man and one woman. Covenants are characterized by a sense of permanency. And when God establishes the terms of a covenant, only God has the authority to change them (Galatians 3:15).

When transitioning from the old (Mosaic) covenant to the new, the Lord clearly announced the change (Acts 10). But He did no such thing with the marriage covenant He had established in the garden paradise of Eden (Genesis 2:24). If anything, Jesus *strengthened* the terms of the marriage covenant that the ancient Jews had weakened (Matthew 19:3–9).

Sex creates a spiritual *oneness* and is intended by God to be covenantal (1 Corinthians 6:9–20). And so it is that any sexual activity outside of the marriage bond is sinful and in violation of God's good design.

Yes, there are situations in which the Lord allows for divorce, and yes, the blood of Jesus can cleanse even the worst sexual sins. But Western culture has played too fast and loose with this issue. Twenty years ago, I would not have listed marriage as a core doctrine, but times have changed and early church leaders made clear this is not something to be treated lightly (Acts 15).

OUR RESPONSE

As we consider these doctrinal standards, we see many organizations function outside their boundaries. That alone is cause for division because humans have no authority to change the core of Christianity.

I am not intending to be harsh, just true to the faith. When I am confronted with Biblical truths that seem at odds with my personal inclinations, I have no choice but to conform to the teachings of the Bible. If I wanted to, I could adapt the Scriptures to fit my opinions, but then I would no longer be practicing Christianity. I would have to invent a new religion such as "Happy Bobism."

The bizarre idea of starting my own religion prompts me to give a word of caution to those considering local church involvement: choose wisely! Not every organization that brandishes the name of God represents Him well. Not every pastor who claims to speak truth presents a clear and accurate understanding of the gospel. And not every congregation that gathers to worship can be considered healthy. Not only do frauds exist, but far too many have also abandoned the foundations of the Christian faith. Even good and well-intentioned believers can make ill-fated and sinful choices. Still, the Lord continues to work powerfully in our day, and we want to align with those who are truly pursuing His purposes.

I can understand how people might struggle with these ideas, including those related to marriage and sexuality. Sexual desires run deep, and the over-sexualization of culture makes the challenges we face even more difficult. But our response plays a vital role in it all.

In times of old, when confronted with their sinfulness, the people of God would tear their clothes, cover themselves with ashes, and fall on their faces in repentance. That is a very different response from rising up in pride and anger because of feeling offended by a Scriptural truth not to our liking. *Meaningful change always begins with getting our hearts right before the Lord.*

I have found *compassion without compromise* to provide the best approach regarding the core doctrines of the Christian faith. As representatives of Christ, we never want to waver in our faithful devotion to the Lord, but neither do we want to heap condemnation on the shoulders of broken people. The apostle Paul said it best: "Such were some of you; but you were washed, but you were sanctified, but you were justified in the name of the Lord Jesus Christ and in the Spirit of our God" (1 Corinthians 6:11).

The Lord has designed His body to be diverse. We are free to adopt different styles and worship as we see fit. We are even free to hold diverse opinions regarding nonessential doctrines. But we are not free to redefine the core elements of the faith according to our own liking.

Inclusivity is not necessarily a Biblical virtue. The creatures before God's throne constantly proclaim, "Holy, holy, holy"—not "Inclusive, inclusive, inclusive" (Revelation 4:8). We would be wise to take note and align our perspectives accordingly.

Digging Deeper
Into Chapter Nineteen

Because of our law-based tendencies, humans have a way of making life more complicated than the Lord intends. We excel at creating layers of rules and standards and then using them to force others into preconceived molds. But apart from the core doctrines of the faith, God gives us far more freedom than we often allow.

In principle, I do not see a problem with churches or denominations celebrating certain "distinctives" they feel compelled to embrace. One might elevate prayer, another community engagement, and still another ministry to the downtrodden. When taken together, these form a beautiful representation of the body of Christ. But any one of these good distinctives can become problematic if it becomes the standard by which we judge other believers.

Christian unity is *covenantal*, meaning it flows from embracing the essentials of our faith.

> *Dig deeper: John 17:17–24*
> *1 Corinthians 1:10–13*

Those who penned New Testament letters repeatedly emphasized the importance of *unity*. Why would this be? They felt compelled to elevate the importance of unity because humanity is ever prone to conflict and division.

> *Dig deeper: Ephesians 4:1–6*

Even today, it seems as though many Christians disregard Scriptural admonitions toward unity in their arguments over doctrinal standards and church practices. I understand their concerns but often disagree with their methods. In this, I find Acts 15 to be of great value in our efforts to understand God's expectations for our lives and ministries.

> *Dig deeper: Acts 15:1–35*

In the early church, many of the Jews and Gentiles did not mix well. The gospel, it seems, confronted perspectives that had been deeply ingrained for centuries. And so it was that some Jewish Christians tried to compel Gentile believers to embrace certain aspects of the Mosaic law—circumcision in particular.

We can glean much from the response by Peter and James and the other early church leaders. If ever there was an opportunity for them to lay out a list of rules for Christian living, this was it. But, wisely, they kept only to the *essentials*. Consider what these pioneers of the faith wrote to the Gentile believers:

> "For it seemed good to the Holy Spirit and to us to lay upon you no greater burden than these essentials: that you abstain from things sacrificed to idols and from blood and from things strangled and from fornication; if you keep yourselves free from such things, you will do well. Farewell." Acts 15:28–29

God had called Gentile Christians out of pagan practices such as worshiping idols, drinking blood, and engaging in sexually immoral activities like temple prostitution and group sex. These were often interconnected with pagan rituals, while each, for its own reason, violated a sacred covenant established by God for human benefit.

So while early church leaders admonished Gentile Christians to make a "clean break" from their pagan lifestyles of the past, they did not feel inclined to place any other burdens on their shoulders. Christian life and unity always work best when we focus on the essentials.

QUESTIONS

1. Why is it reasonable to expect a variety of churches and denominations to exist?
2. Why are the five core doctrines of the faith necessary?
3. What does it mean to have compassion without compromise?
4. Why is Christian unity important to God?
5. What does it mean to say that church unity is covenantal?
6. What do we learn from Acts 15?

Chapter 20
Connected

I do not know when or how the change took place. But if we were to compare a typical church service today with one in New Testament times, we would notice a vast difference. To begin, the first Christians met in homes. Their services were sometimes called "*agape*" (love) feasts, being loosely patterned after the Last Supper. The people of God would share a meal, which included bread and wine in memory of Jesus' death, to celebrate the new covenant in Christ. Through that relational experience, people drew near to the Lord and one another.

In many churches today, a person can sit alone, watch gifted musicians sing, and hear an inspirational message before quietly slipping out once again. I am not criticizing our modern services as nonbiblical, but recognizing the potential of attending regularly without building meaningful relationships. Even worse, some people profess to walk with God but refuse to attend church at all.

The first letter of John helps establish our Biblical perspective:

> What was from the beginning, what we have heard, what we have seen with our eyes, what we have looked at and touched with our hands, concerning the Word of Life—and the life was manifested, and we have seen and testify and proclaim to you the eternal life, which was with the Father and was manifested to us—what we have seen and heard we proclaim to you also, so that you too may have fellowship with us; and indeed our fellowship is with the Father, and with His Son Jesus Christ. These things we write, so that our joy may be made complete. 1 John 1:1–4

Fellowship with God and one another—these have always been at the core of God's design for His church. But it is not just fellowship for the sake of fellowship; together, we exercise the privilege of representing Christ to a world in need.

The original meaning of the Greek word *ekklēsía*—from which our word *church* is derived—was not necessarily religious. It simply referred to an assembly of people who were "called out" for a specific purpose, such as a local government community meeting. Christians chose to adopt a secular concept to help define the collective whole of God's people. In a broad sense, we think of the *church universal*, which consists of all true followers of Christ across the globe. The church, in this sense, is the worldwide assembly of the citizens of God's kingdom whom He calls out from the commonality and corruption of humanity to accomplish His eternal purposes on earth. However, the New Testament writers expected God's people to also gather *locally* for worship, fellowship, and service (Hebrews 10:25).

What we do *not* find in the Bible are any references to physical buildings adorned with steeples and crosses. I cannot imagine us ever changing the terminology to begin calling a church building by another name, but we can rediscover and elevate the original meaning of "church." *Biblically speaking, a church is not a building but a collective gathering of God's people.*

The Bible provides several metaphors for the church to help us better grasp God's intent. Together, they help paint a more complete picture of what the Lord desires for His people.

BRIDE

It might seem strange to some—especially men—that the Bible refers to the church as the *bride* of Christ (2 Corinthians 11:2; Revelation 19:7). How else can we take it than to realize the Lord's deep love for His people? One needs only to contemplate the passionate love between a bride and groom to gain fresh insight regarding Jesus' desire for His church.

FAMILY/HOUSEHOLD

As we acknowledge God to be the most powerful, glorious, and magnificent Being ever to exist, we begin to realize the amazing privilege of using the term "heavenly Father." To be crowned as a child of the King of Glory, there can be no greater honor. And so it is that we are members of God's *household* and bound together as brothers and sisters in Christ. No family is perfect, but family is what we are.

> So then you are no longer strangers and aliens, but you are fellow citizens with the saints, and are of God's household, having been built on the foundation of the apostles and prophets, Christ Jesus Himself being the corner stone, in whom the whole building, being fitted together, is growing into a holy temple in the Lord, in whom you also are being built together into a dwelling of God in the Spirit. Ephesians 2:19–22

TEMPLE

Ephesians 2 also refers to the church as a *temple*. God does not dwell in ornate physical temples like places of worship in the days of old. The Creator of the universe has chosen to dwell in a temple He is building with "living stones" (1 Peter 2:4–8). Bound by love, the people of God collectively become His sacred dwelling place. And while we can pray and worship and walk with God as individual "mini-temples," there will always be ways that the Lord works only through His corporate body. Nowhere in the New Testament do we see it encouraged—or even accepted—to live isolated, individualistic lifestyles.

BODY

The metaphor of Christ's church as His *body* speaks volumes to those who profess His name (1 Corinthians 12:12–27). How does a body function? Interconnected parts obey the commands of the head to work in unison. In this sense, God designed the body of Christ to accomplish specific purposes, and we hold each part in high esteem for its individual role. But no part of the body can act as an isolated entity. Each member complements the others in obedience to the Head.

The church does not exist for itself, to fulfill our personal desires. And though our gatherings should include times of singing as worship, we are also called to influence the world around us as an act of worship.

If we see church attendance as something God expects to complete a religious checklist, we have misunderstood His intent. The Lord calls His church to reach, care for, and help grow people both within and beyond the walls of a building. A church member need not do everything there is to do in a local fellowship, but we should all be playing active roles as we live in obedience to the Lord.

COMMUNITY

Churches are not just located in a community; *churches form a community*. And how we need it in our fractured Western world! Community happens on every level, from pastors building friendships and working together, to business leaders strategizing for local improvement, to healthcare workers banding together to help those in need. Regardless of the specific focus, it is all about developing healthy connections to glorify God and serve humanity.

Of significant concern is that our modern representation of the church seems to fall far short of the Biblical ideal. And while I think I see the shortcomings as well as most, I cannot deny the wisdom of God's design.

Shortcomings of family and church should not give cause for abandoning the concepts, but for strengthening our resolve to return a kingdom mindset. We resolve to honor the Lord and His covenants, to return to the humble principles that make those relationships work. Will we encounter some daunting challenges? Most likely. But if we seek to honor God's covenants, He will guide our efforts.

The church matters to my Lord and Savior, and so the church matters to me. There will always be false prophets, hypocrites, and people who fail to live out the fullness of God's love, but that is no excuse to distance myself from the fellow members of His household.

Developing healthy relational connections within the body of Christ is part of God's plan for our spiritual growth. The teachings of Jesus and His disciples challenge and equip us to work through our disagreements in pursuit of relational health. And as we learn to work through the relational issues that cannot help but arise, we ourselves will mature into the image of Christ. God's design for the church is perfect, even if the various parts of His body are not.

Digging Deeper
Into Chapter Twenty

Why do some people embrace Jesus as the Head but refuse to develop any meaningful connections with His body—the church? I could list ten or twelve reasons, and each one would hold a measure of truth.

Some people have been hurt by the selfish or unethical behavior of church members or leaders. Perhaps they do not trust organized religion. Perhaps the church seems to have an unhealthy focus on money. Perhaps people feel judged the moment they walk through church doors. Perhaps the services feel like performances that are irrelevant to their lives. Perhaps...

Each of these criticisms can be valid in its own way. And having been actively involved for over four decades, I can relate to most of them. I know the pain of being deeply wounded by callous or unethical behavior from those who should be stellar examples of a living faith. But I have also experienced God's redeeming grace through the pain. In each and every circumstance, I not only received the Lord's healing touch, but came away better for the experience.

A major key involves finding a *healthy* local church. No church is perfect because they are all comprised of people, but some provide much better spiritual environments than others.

Online reviews can be a helpful part of the discovery process, but even great churches might have bad reviews given by disgruntled former members or theological enemies of God. A healthy church will focus on honoring God over trying to please everyone.

Dig deeper: John 15:18–25

I suggest checking out a church's *statement of faith* to see how it aligns with New Testament truth. You can also talk with Christian friends, neighbors, and coworkers to get a sense of a church's reputation in a community. After that, it is time to step out of your comfort zone and visit some Sunday services.

Unless you get a clear sense otherwise, I suggest visiting several churches. Do the leaders seem humble and noncontrolling? Does the church feel like a good fit for you? If you suspect an issue might create long-term frustration, it is best to thoroughly consider it now.

If you think the Lord is leading you to a specific church, visit several times to confirm His leading. You want to get your choice settled in your heart. No matter where you land, issues will eventually arise because churches are made of imperfect people.

Faithful attendance and involvement are vital; they help form the necessary ingredients for growth. But that does not mean you can never leave—like we did many years ago.

Our church leaders seemed to have a high degree of devotion to God, but came off as controlling. And though they preached a message of grace, the environment was characterized by a long list of unwritten rules. In spite of the conflicting emotions involved with leaving, I know we made the correct choice. A lot of people came away from that organization both spiritually and emotionally damaged.

No doubt, finding and connecting with a healthy church body will stretch you. But despite the many challenges, church involvement can be one of the greatest blessings of your life—as it has been for mine!

See also: Hebrews 10:19–25

QUESTIONS

1. How would you define *church*?
2. What are some primary purposes of the church?
3. Why is local church involvement necessary?
4. How does church involvement help us grow to maturity?
5. What are some markers of a healthy church?
6. What does it mean to be faithful to a local congregation?

Chapter 21

The Dynamics of Forgiveness

How it happened remains a mystery to me, but our daughter Beth has grown to become a gifted and successful nurse. Do not get me wrong; I never questioned her ability or determination. I simply do not know how she ended up in the field of nursing.

When Beth was about three years old, she tripped and fell on the cement at our public pool. A nasty gash on her small chin meant a trip to the nearby emergency room for stitches. The skinny little three-year-old girl screamed and thrashed so hard that all the hospital's doctors and all the hospital's nurses could not keep her still. And so Dad was called in to assist with the procedure. That experience could have gone better.

Holding my screaming daughter and watching the doctor stitch her chin under a sun-sized light was a bit much for me. And though he swore she felt no pain, I knew differently when Beth let out an extra-loud wail as the needle went a bit too deep. When all was said and done, we left the emergency room with me sitting in a wheelchair and Beth on my lap. The gracious staff gave my little girl stickers and a popsicle. All I got was the bill.

On another occasion, when she was not much older, Beth got a splinter in her hand. No doubt the pain was significant, but the fear of me removing the errant sliver of wood was even worse. Anytime I got a sterilized needle even close to her hand, my little girl would shriek like a pterodactyl caught in a tar pit. She knew as well as I did that the splinter needed to come out, but the "unpleasantness" of the experience compelled her to fight me every step of the way.

Evidently, Beth got over those traumatic experiences, while I did not. Today she is a nurse, and I do my best to keep hospitals at a distance. We are quite proud of our daughter, although I suppose being involved with the medical field is always easier when you are jabbing others with needles instead of being jabbed yourself.

OUT WITH THE BAD

When it comes to the human body, things such as splinters, abscesses, and tumors simply do not belong. Unless they are dealt with and removed, even worse suffering results. Surgery might not be fun, but the pain of a neglected problem is even "less funner." Something similar can be said about our spiritual lives.

Forgiveness is in some ways similar to surgery. While we all like how we feel after the healing takes place, getting to that point is never on our list of favorite activities. Two elements of forgiveness provide different challenges, but both are vital for healthy spiritual and emotional living.

RECEIVING FORGIVENESS FROM GOD

One of the problems with trying to please God through our good works is that we never thoroughly deal with the sins of our past. Sometimes, we try to stuff them away in spiritual closets. And sometimes, we try to bury them under a blanket of good deeds. But the sins—and their spiritual stench—never go away. When the screens go dark and the music grows quiet and the lights go low, hints of that hideous stench begin to waft to our nostrils. And try as we might to mask the odor with good deeds, the smell never quite dissipates.

Only one "cleanser" can make us new: *the blood of Jesus*. But receiving forgiveness for our sins requires bringing them into the light, and that can be an experience most unpleasant. So we try to cover and hide and atone for ourselves, never getting better and never truly moving forward in life.

When we get honest about our failures and shortcomings, feelings of unworthiness begin to surface. That pain, unfortunately, can feel worse than a splinter. Worse still, we tend to avoid God and His people because of an innate awareness of how far we fall short. But avoidance is the worst possible response. What we fail to realize through the haze of emotion is that Jesus died on the cross for the very purpose of forgiving our sins.

There is yet another aspect to the problem of sin that I rarely hear mentioned. When Adam and Eve joined the devil's treasonous rebellion against God, they brought a terrible curse upon humanity (Genesis 3:15–19). The curse hounds us, imbuing even our most noble endeavors with pain and death. One cannot simply shake off the curse the way a dog would rid its fur of water. But when Jesus suffered and died for our sins, He also took the curse upon His innocent head— as symbolized by the crown of thorns pressed upon His brow (John 19:1–3). Then, through His resurrection, Jesus shattered the power of the curse forever.

God does *not* want His extreme sacrifice to be wasted. If you gave someone an expensive gift card, how would you feel if it sat unused in a junk drawer? The smartest, wisest, most loving thing you can do is to humbly bring your sins into the light before God and ask Him to forgive. If you refuse to humble yourself, you will become more miserable with each passing day (Psalm 32:1–7). But once you get to the other side, you will wonder why you ever hesitated. To discover that there is no condemnation for those who are in Christ is to experience freedom and healing like never before (Romans 8:1).

FORGIVING OTHERS

A friend and I once served together in leadership roles at a Christian conference. During a time of evening ministry, we found ourselves speaking with a bitter young man who was contemplating the idea of forgiving his mother for several long-standing offenses. The fellow had been involved with Christian circles for many years, but still nursed a long-held grudge toward the woman who brought him into this world. I do not remember many details of that evening, but one aspect of our conversation left a clear mark: it took him what felt like *forever* to let go and forgive. By the time he finally did, we were all exhausted and done for the night.

That situation was not entirely unique. I can think of several more in which I encouraged a person to forgive and let go. Most of the circumstances ended favorably, but none of the resolutions came quickly. Why is that? Why is it so difficult for us to forgive? Why is it so hard for us to let go?

My heart once seethed with bitterness because of a painful mix of neglect, mistreatment, and envy. Ironically, my hardened heart did more damage to me and those who were close than anyone else. In the days since, I have seen far too many families polluted by a "root of bitterness," as mentioned by the writer of Hebrews:

> Pursue peace with everyone, and holiness—without it no one will see the Lord. Make sure that no one falls short of the grace of God and that no root of bitterness springs up, causing trouble and by it, defiling many. Hebrews 12:14-15 (HCSB)

Jesus established forgiving others as a *requirement* for God forgiving our sins (Matthew 6:14-15). Why would He take an approach that might cause us considerable pain and difficulty? Because it is best for us. The command to forgive others compels us to work through our heart issues—even if haltingly—so our relationship with God can be unhindered. Even more, it challenges our pride as the Lord seeks to redeem and restore our broken relationships. And somehow, in the process, we find healing ourselves. If we will step back and look at the big picture, we will see both the beauty and wisdom of His plan.

Forgiving a person's transgressions against you does not require you to trust that individual, or even to forget what he or she did. But it does mean letting go of the bitter feelings you have been nursing in your heart. To forgive is to *let go*; to remain bitter is to hold on to control—and the fruit is never good.

Bitterness is not worth the price it exacts. It is not worth the misery it invites into our hearts. It is not worth the spiritual blindness it spawns. It is not worth the damage it does to our families. It is not worth a lifetime of unhealthy relationships. Remaining bitter offers no meaningful benefits but leaves us with many regrets.

If you want to truly live, learn the dynamics of forgiveness. Bring your sins into the light of the cross so they can be washed away by the power of Jesus' blood. And forgive those who have hurt you so you can welcome the blessings of God's kingdom into your life, family, and circumstances. I have never heard of anyone who regretted forgiving, but many have lamented nurturing the bitter pill of unforgiveness.

Digging Deeper Into Chapter Twenty-One

Sin tends to run in cycles. And those cycles can become traps from which there seems to be no escape.

Sometimes, the cycles will envelop multiple generations of a family. Perhaps an alcoholic abuses his young son. And despite his vows to the contrary, the boy grows up to be an abusive alcoholic himself.

Within the cycles of familial sin, we also see individuals bound by undesirable—and unwanted—behavior. No amount of self-effort seems to break those shackles, so how can we possibly find freedom?

As much as being forgiven of our sins matters, God does not forgive us so we can continue to repeat bad behavior. He always intends to lead us to a place of freedom. The path might not be straight or simple, but there is hope if we are willing to persist.

To begin, we want to recognize the role of Jesus as our *high priest*—the primary *intercessor* between God and humanity.

> *Dig deeper: Hebrews 4:14–16*

Because Jesus lived in human flesh, and because He took all our sins upon His shoulders on the cross, He understands our struggles. Even better, He died on that cross as a perfect sacrifice that we might be forgiven of all our transgressions. This means that God wants us to draw near even when we are at our worst. And if we are willing to admit our wrongs and humble our hearts, He will welcome us with open arms. *Every time.*

I discovered long ago that attempting to run from the Lord is the most foolish thing we can do. Reliance on self is what gets us into trouble, and reliance on self will never get us out. Instead, we must learn to lean into our Savior's abundant grace.

Grace is unmerited favor from God, and so much more. Grace also provides the *power* we need to break free and live in victory over sin.

Dig deeper: Romans 5:15–21

Guilt and self-condemnation are key components of the cycle of sin. The devil will entice us to do something wrong and then keep us self-focused and defeated by continually reminding us of our failure. Even our own hearts will condemn us. But the Lord is always willing to forgive if we are willing to humble ourselves before His throne.

The key is to confess our sins before God, receive His forgiveness, and hold that forgiveness tight through faith. We fix our eyes on Jesus the Passover Lamb, refusing to accept guilt or self-condemnation.

Dig deeper: Romans 8:1–2

If you continue to struggle without forward progress, if the cycle of sin seems so tight that you can never break free, it is time to take another step of humility by inviting mature and loving Christians into the situation.

Dig deeper: James 5:13–16

Sometimes, just taking the extra step of humility will suffice. And sometimes, a person might need more extensive prayer because of strongholds the devil has established through trauma, involvement with the occult, or other issues. The process will likely not be pain-free, but God's hope shines like the morning sun proclaiming a new day.

QUESTIONS

1. Why do we need to be forgiven by God?
2. Why is it foolish to attempt to run from the Lord?
3. How do we know God wants to forgive our sins?
4. Why is it vital that we forgive others?
5. Why does humility matter when it comes to receiving forgiveness and breaking free from the cycles of sin?
6. What touches you most about Hebrews 4:14–16?

Chapter 22
Manna from Heaven

Thinking back to my childhood, I remember the "Fuller Brush man" who visited our neighborhood selling his wares. He was an older guy whose haircut looked like the edge of a gray cliff rising from his shiny forehead. Parking a station wagon across the street from our house, the man would work his way from door to door selling cleaning supplies.

The Fuller Brush man was not alone—at least in a general sense. Other salespeople also frequented our neighborhood. We lived in low-income housing, but the homes were concentrated with easy access. And I do not think most residents managed their funds well. If there is money to be made, someone will find a way to get the sale.

THE HOLY BIBLE

That was how we came to have a large, cream-colored "Holy Bible" with ornate gold lettering sitting in our living room. My mother thought the Bible would be a nice addition to our home, so she helped to pad someone's paycheck.

Mom has long since passed, but I still have that Bible—with cracked spine and old tape marks. Inside it reads: "this HOLY BIBLE presented to: Rosalie Santos by Master Piece Family Bible on February 27, 1971". With her name, the name of the Bible company, and the date in blue marker, I do not think Mom quite grasped the intent of the presentation page. And considering the February date on which she purchased it, my mother might have just felt sorry for someone trudging through the frigid air and deep snowdrifts of western Pennsylvania to help pay heating bills.

Inside, I found a few reminders of my mother's faith life. A card from my father's funeral, a Catholic poem (she was not Catholic, though), a newspaper clipping about positive thinking, and a fundraising card from a televangelist (with her name spelled wrong) saying, "You are a beautiful person!" There was also a cutout from the back of a church bulletin titled "LET THE WORD OF GOD DO ITS WORK!"

> If you are cold, let it WARM you,
> If you are asleep, let it WAKE you,
> If you are a backslider, let it WARN you,
> If you are defiled, let it WASH you,
> If you are disobedient, let it WHIP you,
> If you are uncertain, let it WITNESS to you,
> If you are unsaved, let it WIN you.[1]

My mother struggled in life. Immensely. With minimal education, little money, a sickly husband, and a rebellious teenage son, the cards of life seemed stacked against her. But amid the trouble and brokenness, Mom had a practice that has also stuck with me all these years: leaning into God through His Word. She especially loved the Psalms—likely because she could relate well to the emotional highs and lows expressed through their verses.

The Bible is the most profound book ever penned. A person with a sixth-grade education—like my mother—can draw sweet nectar of life from its pages. And a college graduate with a degree in chemistry—like me—can be transformed by the depths of wisdom contained within. No matter where you lie on the education-intelligence continuum, the Bible is your gateway to the God who spoke our cosmos into existence with but a few simple words.

The Bible is heaven's spiritual logic expressed to humanity, but not all humans have learned to draw life from its pages. For the proud and stubborn, the Bible's transformational wisdom remains hidden in an impenetrable vault. Sure, they can find nuggets of insight, inspiration for the day, and morals to live by, but grasping the depths of God's logic comes only through the Holy Spirit. And while His wisdom remains available to all, the state of a person's heart means everything.

In what seems like profound irony, the pages of the Bible abound with mystery, but no "secret society" owns insight into those truths.

---

1. I do not know the source of this poem, but based on the use of alliteration and the letter "W," I am assuming it was written by a pastor as part of his seven-point sermon.

Certainly, we can draw upon the work of scholars who have spent countless hours in academic study. But make no mistake, the Holy Spirit does not limit His wisdom to those with theology degrees. If we are willing to humble ourselves, seek His truth, and align with His ways, He is willing to open our eyes to a grand reality far surpassing the scope of our natural vision.

THE BREAD OF ANGELS

As descendants of God's friend Abraham, the people of ancient Israel suffered for several hundred years in slavery under the cruel hand of the Egyptian pharaoh. God had not forgotten them, nor did their prayers for help go unheard (Exodus 3:7–9). But the Lord seemed slow to act because He was allowing a powerful plan for their deliverance to unfold. When that time finally arrived, Moses led hundreds of thousands of people out of Egypt and into a barren wilderness. In miraculous fashion, the Lord divided the Red Sea to save their lives, caused water to spring from barren rocks to satisfy their thirsts, and sent *manna* from heaven to feed their bodies.

Manna was a fine, edible substance—like flour—that could be baked into a bread. Through forty years of wilderness wanderings, God fed the people of Israel with the bread of angels. And when they finally arrived at the border of the Promised Land, through Moses the Lord provided a much-needed perspective of their experience:

> "You shall remember all the way which the LORD your God has led you in the wilderness these forty years, that He might humble you, testing you, to know what was in your heart, whether you would keep His commandments or not. He humbled you and let you be hungry, and fed you with manna which you did not know, nor did your fathers know, that He might make you understand that man does not live by bread alone, but man lives by everything that proceeds out of the mouth of the LORD." Deuteronomy 8:2–3

Jesus quoted the last part of this passage while responding to the devil's temptations in the wilderness. As the Lord fasted for forty days, the devil enticed Him with bread. How did Jesus respond?

"Man shall not live on bread alone, but on every word that proceeds out of the mouth of God." Matthew 4:4b

Spiritual life requires spiritual food, and regardless of how much we profess to love God, our spiritual strength will wane if we do not routinely dine at the table of His Word. If you want a spiritually vibrant life, you *must* develop a habit of spending time daily in God's Word. No universal formula exists for how much or how long, but the nourishment of Scripture will always be essential to our well-being.

GETTING STARTED

Controversy and confusion abound regarding the number of Bible versions, but I see the diversity as a gift from God. When selecting a version for personal use, I recommend finding a balance between *accuracy* and *readability*.[2] And you will want to look for a *translation* rather than a *paraphrase*. Reliable translations are the work of multiple scholars trained in the original languages of the Bible. A paraphrase is usually the work of one person. Paraphrases might be readable, poetic, and inspiring, but I see them as "desserts" more than main meals.

Deciding where to start reading in the Bible can also be confusing. I love the book of Genesis, but many well-meaning people have seen their spiritual thirst turn to drought as they struggled to work through the pages of the Mosaic law. Thus, I find it best to begin with the Gospel of Luke or John, returning to the Old Testament when you are a little more seasoned in the Word. And each time you begin reading, remember to petition God for wisdom and insight into His truth.

One of the many bright spots in the Western world today is that Biblical resources abound. If you truly want to learn how to navigate the pages of the Bible, there are plenty of websites, books, videos, and church people for you to draw upon.

I once saw the Bible as an alien book in an unreadable language. Today, I am writing books about spiritual truths. If you have a heart to learn, God will teach you and nourish your soul in the process!

---

2. "Comparison Chart of Bible Translations Showing Style or Type of Translation and Readability or Grade Level," Not Just Another Book!, accessed February 18, 2025, https://www.notjustanotherbook.com/biblecomparison.htm.

Digging Deeper
Into Chapter Twenty-Two

I think it safe to assume that the conversation between Jesus and Pontius Pilate was tense. The Rome-appointed governor of Judea had been thrust into an uncomfortable position. He recognized Jesus' innocence, but political forces were compelling him to bring condemnation nonetheless.

Dig deeper: John 18:31–40

When Jesus said He came to testify of truth, Pilate ended the conversation with a haunting question: "What is truth?" We might not use Pilate's exact words, but we all ask his question. Much of our anxiety in life stems from not knowing who or what to believe.

Truth is reality. And we mostly consider that reality on two different levels: physical and spiritual. Science pursues an understanding of our natural reality and theology an understanding of our spiritual reality. Science focuses primarily on the question of "how?", while theology addresses the "why?" And how we need the why!

Factors such as money, fear, and selfish desire can all skew our perspectives. And so it is that "my truth" and "your truth" are simply our *perceptions* of reality. But those perceptions can be entirely wrong because appearances can be deceiving.

A friend once asked Debi to borrow her car. While making a left turn across traffic, the friend perceived an oncoming car to be farther than it actually was. "Her truth" at that moment led to a heavily damaged front fender. Thankfully, no one came away injured.

Our goal should be to perceive reality as it is, not as we want it to be. A selfless pursuit of truth enabled Jesus to see and speak with clarity.

See also: John 5:30–32

Why is daily Bible reading so important? It enables our minds, day by day, to be renewed by God's reality. This daily renewal then brings real and lasting transformation to our lives.

Dig deeper: Romans 12:1–2

Simply reading the Bible, however, is not enough. We must also follow the example of Jesus by laying aside personal desires and agendas to allow the truth of God's Word to speak for itself.

Considering the *context* of what we read is also integral to learning. The Bible can be made to say just about anything we want if we pull verses out of the context in which they were written.

Sadly, "proof texting" is a common practice even among devout Christians. It involves isolating Bible verses from their context to provide "proof" for an argument or perspective.

Consider 1 Corinthians 15:22: "For as in Adam all die, so also in Christ all will be made alive." Apart from its context, this verse seems to say all people will eventually be saved. But if we read it within the context of the entire New Testament, we realize it speaks only of Christians.

Wisdom dictates that verses of Scripture should always be considered in context with the cultural mindsets of the day, the history of the era, and what is written in the rest of the Bible—and especially the surrounding verses. A good study Bible can also help with these efforts.

The learning process might feel overwhelming at times, but ours is a journey of grand discovery. How our God wants to teach us His ways!

QUESTIONS

1. Why must we feed daily on the truth of the Bible?
2. Why is a humble heart vital to our spiritual learning process?
3. Why is faith also essential to this process?
4. What do you think of the idea that truth is reality?
5. Why must we be objective in our pursuit of truth?
6. Why is it necessary to consider the context of a verse or passage?

Chapter 23
The Gift of Prayer

Do you think the heavenly Father heard Jesus' prayers? The Lord ensured there would be no doubt in our minds about the answer. And the story is one for the ages.

Lazarus, a close friend of Jesus, had died, his body rotting in the grave for four days. Understandably, Lazarus' sisters were upset. They even expressed anger toward Jesus for ignoring their pleas to come sooner. If the Lord had been there, He could have healed the man and saved everyone considerable grief. But Jesus delayed. And Lazarus died. And his family grieved.

The process of decomposition is not pretty. Within the first three days, the internal organs decay. Then the body begins to bloat from the creation of various gases. And the stench becomes horrid. It was at this stage that Jesus finally arrived on the scene.

To everyone's amazement, the Lord ordered the stone removed from the entrance of Lazarus' burial chamber. Then He prayed:

> "Father, I thank You that You have heard Me. I knew that You always hear Me; but because of the people standing around I said it, so that they may believe that You sent Me." When He had said these things, He cried out with a loud voice, "Lazarus, come forth." The man who had died came forth, bound hand and foot with wrappings, and his face was wrapped around with a cloth. Jesus said to them, "Unbind him, and let him go." John 11:41b–44

I do not suppose those were normal doings in the little village of Bethany. The word spread far and wide, with people coming to see firsthand the man whose decomposing body was now living and breathing like nothing had ever happened.

PRAYERS TO HEAVEN

It is understandable that the heavenly Father would hold Jesus in high regard; He was the sinless Son of God. But what about us? What about those whose histories have been marked by selfish living and repeated failures? What can we expect? Amazingly, the same treatment as Christ!

Our eyes begin to open as we recognize God's deep love for us:

> "The glory which You have given Me I have given to them, that they may be one, just as We are one; I in them and You in Me, that they may be perfected in unity, so that the world may know that You sent Me, and loved them, even as You have loved Me." John 17:22–23

Can you imagine the heavenly Father loving you as much as He loves Jesus? If not, you lack an understanding of God. Our Creator existed long before humanity, and what we do can never influence who He is.

We read in 1 John 4:8 that "God is love." Perfect love *always* characterizes our Creator. It does not matter who you are or what you have done. The idea seems counterintuitive, but God's love for you has more to do with Him than with you. Even when you are at your worst, the Lord still loves you without hesitation. But the good news does not stop there!

Virtually all the benefits extended by heaven to Jesus become ours through the new covenant. We receive favor beyond what we can comprehend, and the Lord promises never to fail or abandon us—no matter how low we sink. And, just like Jesus, we can lift our prayers to heaven with confidence that He will hear. Only in this light can we understand prayer not as a ritual or obligation, but a means of intimate communication with our heavenly Father. Just imagine—a direct line between you and the Almighty Creator at any time and without notice!

These ideas might run contrary to what you have been told, but you will not find a conflicting perspective within the pages of the New Testament. Apart from God the Father *to whom we pray*, Jesus as the *intercessor* between the Father and humanity, and the Holy Spirit as our *advocate*, we need not seek the help of anyone else in heaven.

Perhaps the most "rational" opposing argument is that God has so many prayers ascending to heaven that He needs someone to help share the load—like an administrative assistant who directs calls, depending on their importance. Or maybe we are not worthy enough for our prayers to be heard, and so we need to funnel them through someone with a better moral history. These ideas might feel right, but they do not accurately reflect the teachings of the New Testament.

God created our universe containing a hundred billion galaxies with a hundred billion stars in each. He knows, at every moment, what is happening in every place. So while my mind struggles to comprehend how the Lord could hear billions of prayers at the same time, based on who He is and what He has done, the idea is entirely reasonable.

That we might think ourselves unworthy is understandable. It concerns me more when a person feels worthy of God's approval. But the good news of the kingdom firmly establishes our favor with the heavenly Father through the sacrificial death of Jesus on the cross. If we stay at a distance because of our feelings, we squander the price Jesus paid on our behalf. *Always, we approach the Lord with confidence not because of our worthiness, but because of His.*

> Therefore, since we have a great high priest who has passed through the heavens, Jesus the Son of God, let us hold fast our confession. For we do not have a high priest who cannot sympathize with our weaknesses, but One who has been tempted in all things as we are, yet without sin. Therefore let us draw near with confidence to the throne of grace, so that we may receive mercy and find grace to help in time of need. Hebrews 4:14–16

This passage provides an amazing window into God's heart, along with the purpose of Christ's mission. Jesus paid an extreme price so we might draw near to God's presence without hindrance or barrier.

WHAT PRAYER IS AND IS NOT

Prayer is an act of communion between a person and the God who brought us into existence. And because the Lord is near, a line of communication always remains open. If anything ever hinders our connection with the Lord through prayer, it is on our end and not His. All too often, feelings of doubt or unworthiness prevent us from coming to Him. But as powerful as feelings can be, they have no lasting substance. That is why the truth of God's Word matters so much. Truth always prevails over feelings, and in no arena does that hold more true than with prayer.

Prayer is not about trying to measure up to a standard of holy eloquence or following an exact ritual to perfection. Can you imagine a father forcing his child to conform to rituals to communicate with him? "Okay, son. If you want to approach me, you must first kneel three times and then kiss my ring." Welcoming the kingdom of God through prayer is intended to be an act of the heart.

The purpose of the new covenant is for us to abide in God's presence and communicate with Him freely. It does not matter if your words are smooth or stuttered; the Lord wants to hear from you. And I have found Him to be a much better listener than anyone else I know!

Prayer is also an amazing *privilege*. God does not listen to everyone's prayers. Only those who become His children through faith in Christ are favored to have His ear. Those in the world can expect no such opportunity—unless they approach Him with humble repentance.

PRAYERS WELCOME HEAVEN

Our Savior has not abandoned us to a cold, cruel, and out-of-control world to eke out a miserable existence. He has given us the gift of prayer, and to pray is to welcome heaven to earth.

Heaven comes to earth not through political influence, government laws, or religious rules. Heaven comes to earth as we yield to the Lord's will and invite Him, by faith and love, through the gift of prayer, to work and move in our spheres. What an opportunity heaven's King has given us to draw near to Him and influence the people of this world!

May the Lord grant us wisdom, faith, and courage to move beyond viewing prayer merely as a ritualistic obligation. The gift of prayer provides an opportunity for us to draw near to our divine King and to influence the people and events of the planet on which we live.

Digging Deeper Into Chapter Twenty-Three

No doubt, the Lord will be there for us during times of need, but the benefits of prayer go far beyond our small spheres. Jesus repeatedly proclaimed the good news of the kingdom of God, and it was with a kingdom mindset that He taught His disciples to pray:

> "Our Father who is in heaven,
> Hallowed be Your name.
> "Your kingdom come.
> Your will be done,
> On earth as it is in heaven.
> "Give us this day our daily bread.
> "And forgive us our debts, as we also have forgiven our debtors.
> "And do not lead us into temptation, but deliver us from evil. For Yours is the kingdom and the power and the glory forever. Amen."
> Matthew 6:9b–13

Some treat this prayer as a required ritual to recite, but that was the very thing Jesus cautioned against (Matthew 6:7–8). The Lord's Prayer is more a *model* than a ritual, providing glimmering hints of how the kingdom functions.

The Lord's Prayer begins by establishing our *focus*. People are naturally self-centered, and we are inclined to make life about us. And so we build our own kingdoms—sometimes in God's name. Our world is also full of distractions, which pull our attention in a thousand different directions. Making God central is the beginning of everything good.

Not only did Jesus teach us to establish our focus, He also taught us to *establish a kingdom environment* through worship. God does not need our worship; He is not a glory seeker since He is the source of all glory. When we worship the Lord, we are aligning with the reality of the universe. Our holy Creator is the center of the cosmos and the source of all goodness. To worship is to align with reality. To align is to welcome His presence, and to welcome His presence is to create a kingdom environment.

See also: Psalm 148

Yielding to God's will is another integral aspect of prayer. I cannot begin to tell you how many people pray to a god of their own creation. But if we want the blessings of the kingdom of God, we must welcome the kingdom. And the only way to welcome the kingdom is to welcome the King. I am not referring to a god conceived by our natural affinities, but the real God—the sovereign Almighty who rules and reigns above all.

Surrendering control—whether by yielding or letting go of bitterness—means everything when it comes to welcoming God's rule. Jesus also modeled how to yield in the most extreme circumstances imaginable.

Dig deeper: Luke 22:39–44

The idea of *dependence* upon God might strike fear into the hearts of some people, but it is also integral to kingdom living. Regardless of whether we realize it, we are always dependent upon our Creator; Jesus was simply calling us to acknowledge and proclaim the reality of our circumstances. Thankfully, being dependent upon God is the best situation for any of us because the Lord is always faithful!

QUESTIONS

1. What do you think about the heavenly Father loving you as much as He loves Jesus?
2. What are some benefits we receive through faith in Christ?
3. Why is Jesus the perfect intercessor between God and humanity?
4. Why is it foolish to run from God because we feel unworthy?
5. How does the Lord's Prayer help us establish a kingdom environment?
6. How can you better align with God through the Lord's Prayer?

Chapter 24
The End Is the Beginning

In 1947, a group of very concerned nuclear scientists created the "Doomsday Clock." The Clock was designed to symbolize the potential for a global catastrophe due to threats from man-made technologies. At that time, the threat of a nuclear war loomed large as the United States and the Soviet Union engaged in an arms race. In more recent years, those who adjust the Clock's time have added potential threats from climate change and AI to the mix of international concerns. As technological advancements have multiplied, the Doomsday Clock has crept closer to the proverbial midnight hour when all hell breaks loose.

If I were prone to lying awake at night fretting about our world ending, I would also think about other potential disasters. The Pacific Ring of Fire, for instance, looks like a catastrophe just waiting to happen. Several tectonic plates meet around the rim of the Pacific Ocean, which makes the region ripe for volcanoes, earthquakes, and tsunamis. Compared to other areas, the Ring of Fire holds the most active volcanoes and possesses the greatest threat of a massive eruption. History tells us that 1816 holds the unfortunate title of "the year without summer" because of the devastating effects of a major eruption of Mount Tambora in Indonesia. If multiple volcanoes were to erupt at once, the fallout would rival anything seen in movies.

Weather-related events have also become of increasing concern with intense droughts, windstorms, and floods seemingly on the increase. A person need not live long to be touched by one of these natural disasters. And let us not forget the potential for calamity from space! Many scientists believe a massive comet took out the dinosaurs. How can we be sure it will not happen to us? And what about solar storms? Aside from providing the gorgeous northern lights, a major solar flare could destroy satellites and their GPS capabilities, render computer chips nonfunctional, and bring down electrical grids. Virtually everyone would be affected.

SLEEP WELL

Now that I have laid out a list of calamities that might come upon our planet, will you anxiously toss and turn tonight? There is no need! I share all these things not to frighten you, but to help paint a picture.

We grasp for a sense of permanency in this world, but that idea has always been a myth. Our bodies, and even the world surrounding us, function in a state of constant flux. And the rise of new technologies has increased the pace of change, leaving us feeling anxious and unsettled. Of course, the seeming degradation of human character has not helped. "What is this world coming to?" we might ask. But there is no way we can go back to what once was.

I am not in denial about the potential dangers we face, but I see a *Higher Power* at work. Our world has its insecurities; that remains true. But we are not here by chance, and God reigns over all creation. He created us with plans and purposes that will come to pass by His loving hand. Everything is moving toward a desired end, and though the process will not be pain-free, a glorious future awaits.

Allow me to remind you of Daniel 2:44:

> In the days of those kings the God of heaven will set up a kingdom which will never be destroyed, and that kingdom will not be left for another people; it will crush and put an end to all these kingdoms, but it will itself endure forever. Daniel 2:44

KINGDOM AMBASSADORS

Since the time of Jesus, the kingdom of God has been advancing on earth. And heaven's King has commissioned those who profess the name of Christ to serve as *ambassadors* for that kingdom:

> Now all these things are from God, who reconciled us to Himself through Christ and gave us the ministry of reconciliation, namely, that God was in Christ reconciling the world to Himself, not

counting their trespasses against them, and He has committed to us the word of reconciliation.

Therefore, we are ambassadors for Christ, as though God were making an appeal through us; we beg you on behalf of Christ, be reconciled to God. 2 Corinthians 5:18–20

Jesus was the Messiah long awaited by the ancient Jews, but not the one wanted by most. Many in our modern world carry a similar mindset. We want to believe in a good God. We want to find peace and security through faith. And we want love to characterize our human relationships. Of course, the Lord offers all these things, but none of it comes on our terms or according to our expectations. And so we grasp tightly to our own way. Still, God remains undaunted. The Lord will do what the Lord will do; He does not need our approval.

Due to human sins, our just Creator will bring a cataclysmic judgment at the end of the age, but that is not at all His desire. And so the Lord enlists us to be *ambassadors for Christ* and *ministers of reconciliation*. Though not needing our approval, God does desire our participation in bringing kingdom life to others.

If you are looking for a sense of purpose, this is where to find it. *Whether you work in retail or government or construction, your ultimate purpose involves joining with other members of Christ's body to bear witness of His name and His good kingdom.* Everyone brings different abilities to the table, and everyone plays a unique role, but we all work together to advance God's kingdom on earth by reaching and blessing others with His love, truth, and provision. *We find true meaning as we seek to impart eternal blessings to others.*

PART OF A GOOD PLAN

When all is said and done, when God's purposes on earth have been fulfilled, Jesus will return with great glory. But He will not come as a "suffering servant" this time around. Jesus will return as the "victorious King" to vanquish His foes and claim His rightful rule. Until that day, we need not fear the end of the world. Yes, evil abounds, but even wickedness will become a servant to good in the end.

Some people believe the Lord is waiting for evil to come to full fruition before He returns, but I think the perceived delay has more to do with His desire to flood heaven with people from every nation, tribe, and tongue (2 Peter 3:8-9).

> This gospel of the kingdom shall be preached in the whole world as a testimony to all the nations, and then the end will come.
> Matthew 24:14

I cannot say I understand how everything is going to transpire at the end of our age. Much of it is beyond me. But I see a basic plan unfolding. People are lost and rebellious and in need of Jesus. And as ambassadors for Christ, the Lord is calling us to positively influence their eternal destinies through our prayers, words, and actions.

This God-given mission sounds noble, meaningful, and fulfilling, and it is indeed all these things. But we also face a significant challenge that we dare not overlook: the gospel of the kingdom offends human sensibilities.

We want to be at center stage, for the world to revolve around us. We want to be in control and are unwilling to yield to a higher authority. And if you remember the Great Temptation to seek glory, we want to see ourselves and our beliefs as good—especially if they have been passed to us by our ancestors. Some of us cannot imagine accepting the idea that our family beliefs miss the mark of God's truth. So it is that humans naturally perceive the good news of the kingdom as a threat. And, sometimes for no other reason than our devotion to the Biblical Jesus, there will be people who hate us with a passion.

How we need the profound wisdom of the prophet Daniel, the unshakable faith of Father Abraham and the persistent courage of Paul the apostle! We must keep our eye on the grand scheme of life, nurturing our Lord's desires and seeing by faith the fulfillment of God's eternal purposes. When the dust of this world has cleared and the suffering abated, the Lord will raise His people to a glorious eternity in the Paradise of His presence.

Heaven's King is calling us to put off the old and put on the new because what many perceive as the end will be just the beginning.

Digging Deeper Into Chapter Twenty-Four

It began with the creation of humankind. And despite an almost overwhelming amount of criticism, the Lord has not changed His plan since. I am referring to the vital role we play on this planet called "Earth." The very first words spoken by God about humanity set it all in motion:

> Then God said, "Let Us make man in Our image, according to Our likeness; and let them rule over the fish of the sea and over the birds of the sky and over the cattle and over all the earth, and over every creeping thing that creeps on the earth." God created man in His own image, in the image of God He created him; male and female He created them. God blessed them; and God said to them, "Be fruitful and multiply, and fill the earth, and subdue it; and rule over the fish of the sea and over the birds of the sky and over every living thing that moves on the earth."
> Genesis 1:26–28

From the beginning, the Creator of heaven and earth designated humans to be *stewards* (i.e., managers) of this planet. Distinct from animal life in value and purpose, we have been honored and blessed to rule over earthly affairs. This is God's design, which He has chosen not to alter despite our many shortcomings and failures.

The Almighty gave humans the task of stewarding our globe, but we surrendered that stewardship to the devil, unleashing a powerful torrent of evil. Practically every form of life has suffered as a result.

What was the Lord's solution to redeem our failure? Jesus became a human Himself, overcoming sin and evil through the victorious life intended for Adam and Eve and all humanity. Through His sinless perfection, Jesus reclaimed our stewardship. That is why the role of His church is so important.

Jesus has commissioned His church to fulfill the spiritual stewardship of His kingdom on earth. It is the church that stands against evil to destroy the works of the devil and to advance God's kingdom throughout the world. All of this points to a specific word that carries profound meaning for each of us: *purpose.*

If God does not exist, if this natural world is all there is, we have no lasting purpose. Planet Earth is nothing more than an obscure piece of rock in a meaningless solar system dwarfed by an immense cosmos.

But God does exist, and He has designed us to fulfill meaningful roles in our era. All our gifts and abilities play into the process, as do our life experiences—even those marked by pain and failure. In His wisdom, the Lord will use them all to influence human lives for eternity.

The church is Christ's body, and Jesus the Head gives each part of the body an eternal purpose to fulfill. And though the parts differ from one another, none are considered greater or more significant.

> *Dig deeper: 1 Corinthians 12:14–27*
> *Romans 12:1–13*

Each member of Christ's body is unique and serves a specific role to touch lives and advance God's purposes. This design plays out in communities across the globe, with each church intended to complement the others, and individual members working together in harmony. Please do not allow broken people to distort your perspective of God's good design for you and His beloved church.

QUESTIONS

1. What makes our perceived end just the beginning?
2. What does it mean to be an ambassador for Christ?
3. How can we find meaning and purpose in life?
4. In what ways does the gospel offend human sensibilities?
5. What is the significance of God giving humans stewardship of Planet Earth?
6. How is your life meant to complement the body of Christ?

Chapter 25
Resurrection Life!

Have you ever wished you could get a new body? The idea intrigues me. My current body has sufficed, but it is not one I would have chosen. Chiseled chin, sculpted abs, and stellar hand-eye coordination would all be on my wish list.

If we could exchange our bodies periodically, I suppose we would need to limit the frequency because people might have a difficult time identifying us. Perhaps every ten years—to be accompanied by a birthday party and new unveiling—might be the best option. Or maybe we could just surprise friends and family. But what if my wife detested the changes? That could make life especially difficult.

By managing periodic body exchanges wisely, a person could live forever. But that might not be a great idea in this crazy, mixed-up world. And you can be sure that people would find a way to create a "new body" hierarchy. The rich would hire designer creators and the very poor would get stuck with knock-off models from big box stores that nobody else wants. It would all come down to money, because in the end, that is the way our world functions.

Well, um, perhaps I have seen too many science-fiction movies. It might be best to just forget the idea of body exchanges!

RESURRECTION FROM THE DEAD

When we are young and strong and vibrant, we think we will live forever. But as we age, the realization of life's fragility sets in. I am not sure how it happens, but one day a person wakes up aware that his or her supply of sunrises is running low with no means of replenishment. But death as we know it is not really death; Jesus referred to it simply as "falling asleep" (John 11:11–14). Real death is wrapped up in eternal judgment apart from God, but those who embrace Jesus as the Savior

King will rise to new life and eternal bodies without flaw or weakness. The key theme here is *resurrection*, and it sets Christianity apart from every other religion.

I will admit; some other faiths have a belief in the idea of rising from the dead. But with Christianity, it is established as a historical reality. The reality of Christ's resurrection changes everything!

When Jesus rose after dying as the Passover Lamb sacrificed for human sins, He pioneered a new path. The Son of God did what no mere human ever could; He cheated death. And really, "cheated" is a poor choice of words because He *triumphed* over death, shattering the power of Adam's curse. Try as it might, the grave could not hold Him.

The apostle Paul was once an enemy and persecutor of the church, but an encounter with the living Christ changed his perspective forever:

> For I delivered to you as of first importance what I also received, that Christ died for our sins according to the Scriptures, and that He was buried, and that He was raised on the third day according to the Scriptures, and that He appeared to Cephas, then to the twelve. After that He appeared to more than five hundred brethren at one time, most of whom remain until now, but some have fallen asleep; then He appeared to James, then to all the apostles; and last of all, as to one untimely born, He appeared to me also. 1 Corinthians 15:3–8

"As of first importance." Those who want to know God must begin with the issues that matter most. And Jesus' resurrection from the dead tops the list. Without the resurrection, there really is no Christianity, and apart from a living Christ, we have no hope. If you still have doubts about the Christian faith, I encourage you to research the historical evidence for the resurrection of Jesus Christ.

Jesus' followers were honest people, and many died as martyrs because they would not abandon their claims to have seen the risen Christ. Regardless of the cost, they clung tenaciously to their witness of Christ's victory over the grave. Rightly did they understand that because death could not hold their Lord and Savior, their own bodies—and those of their believing loved ones—would one day rise too.

Throughout the course of my existence, I have attended more funerals than I would have liked. Some of those people went to the grave after a long, full life here on earth. Others were taken at far too young an age. Loved ones always grasp for hope during these times, and some sink into despair. Even amid the worst tragedies, though, I have watched families process their loss with grace because of their confidence in resurrection life. In those grief-filled moments, the reality of a living Christ makes all the difference.

THE PRICE OF FAITH

People often want the benefits of Christianity without being willing to suffer the cost of following Jesus. Some of us even make what sounds like a reasonable argument for the Christian faith: "If I am wrong about Jesus, I will go to my grave and really nothing has been lost. But if you are wrong about Jesus, you are staring at eternity apart from God." Let us contrast this statement with another of the apostle Paul's:

> If we have put our hope in Christ for this life only, we should be pitied more than anyone. 1 Corinthians 15:19 (HCSB)

Paul and many others had paid *extreme* prices for their devotion to the Lord in godless cultures. The world detests the idea of accountability to a sovereign God, and so it maligns His kingdom ambassadors. Kingdoms of devils and men do not take kindly to the rise of an eternal King—or those who serve Him faithfully. Even when physical persecution is not common, serving the Lord still exacts a price through a surrendered will and other hardships created by service to humanity.

But these things should never deter us! We look toward the day when all will bow before the throne of heaven's King. He will reward some with honor and banish others to judgment, which means that what happens here sets the stage for what will happen there.

For those who have suffered in their devotion to Jesus, the resurrection communicates an unshakable hope:

> Now I say this, brethren, that flesh and blood cannot inherit the kingdom of God; nor does the perishable inherit the

> imperishable. Behold, I tell you a mystery; we will not all sleep, but we will all be changed, in a moment, in the twinkling of an eye, at the last trumpet; for the trumpet will sound, and the dead will be raised imperishable, and we will be changed. For this perishable must put on the imperishable, and this mortal must put on immortality. But when this perishable will have put on the imperishable, and this mortal will have put on immortality, then will come about the saying that is written, "Death is swallowed up in victory." 1 Corinthians 15:50–54

I do not understand why we grasp the things of this world so tightly. Nothing on our planet will endure. Still, we exhaust ourselves accumulating material wealth, only to realize the vanity as our final breaths expire. And how often do we compromise our beliefs for human approval, not realizing the rewards we forfeit? Time on this earth is very short, and eternity very long.

Of course, apart from Christ's resurrection, I would present none of these arguments. But I spy something in the distance: a day when these frail bodies rise from the dust to be transformed by the eternal power of God. It will be a day, according to the astute apostle Paul, when the perishable puts on the imperishable, and the mortal puts on immortality.

I do not know where you are today or what issues plague you. I do not know what physical challenges you face or how you have been treated by others. I do not know what hardships you have experienced or how many times you have stumbled. But this I know: *those who embrace Jesus as Lord and Savior will one day rise to eternal glory.* On that day, soon to be, the hardships of this world will fade like distant dreams.

Salvation itself is without cost, but I would be lying if I tried to tell you there was not a price involved with following Jesus (Luke 9:23–27). The real question is whether the sacrifice made is worth the value gained. In Jesus' mind there was no question. He freely paid the most extreme price on our behalf. The reality of the resurrection communicates a blessed future for us too. Because He rose, we also will rise. No price is too steep to pay for the glorious King who awaits us!

Digging Deeper
Into Chapter Twenty-Five

People often question what makes Christianity different from other religions. And while several answers can be given, Christ's resurrection stands out as one of the more significant differences.

Other religious leaders have died and decayed in the grave. But what happened to Jesus was unique in every way. Not only did the Son of God suffer and die for the sins of humanity, He also rose from the dead to shatter the power of sin and death. And while some regard Christ's story as a fictional myth, it all transpired within the backdrop of recorded human history.

The apostle Peter, not long after cowering in fear over the accusations of a slave girl (Matthew 26:69–75), boldly proclaimed the reality of Christ's resurrection before thousands of people.

Dig deeper: Acts 2:22–24

The fact that death could not hold Jesus creates meaning beyond measure! If life in this world is all there is, what can we expect? To accumulate as much wealth as possible? To extract as much pleasure as we can? To be ripped from the presence of our loved ones by the harsh reality of death? To suffer under the weight of poverty, sickness, or injustice only to disappear into nothingness? To sink to the grave without meaning or future?

For Christians, our short time on earth is by no means the sum total of our lives. All we experience here—including pain, abuse, and injustice—is preparing the way for a glorious tomorrow. How well the apostle Paul proclaimed this truth:

> Therefore we do not lose heart, but though our outer man is decaying, yet our inner man is being renewed day by day. For momentary, light affliction is producing for us an eternal weight

> of glory far beyond all comparison, while we look not at the things which are seen, but at the things which are not seen; for the things which are seen are temporal, but the things which are not seen are eternal. 2 Corinthians 4:16–18

Paul also penned inspiring words of eternal hope to the church in Colossae:

> Therefore if you have been raised up with Christ, keep seeking the things above, where Christ is, seated at the right hand of God. Set your mind on the things above, not on the things that are on earth. For you have died and your life is hidden with Christ in God. When Christ, who is our life, is revealed, then you also will be revealed with Him in glory. Colossians 3:1–4

What timely words for this era in which we live! This world is experiencing an upheaval seemingly like never before. How should we respond? By rising to the occasion and fulfilling our God-given purposes for this age. But it is not something we do alone or by our own abilities. Empowered by the Holy Spirit of grace, we join with other believers to advance the kingdom of God and influence others for eternity.

We do not serve for the sake of reward, but it helps to know the Lord values sacrificial service and will richly reward His faithful servants in the next life. And perhaps more importantly, the people we touch in this world will stand at heaven's gates to one day welcome us with grateful appreciation for our sacrifices on their behalf.

QUESTIONS

1. What is significant about Christ's resurrection?
2. How does the resurrection of Jesus lessen the sting of death?
3. How does today's pain pave the way for tomorrow's glory?
4. What is the cost of truly following Christ?
5. How does the resurrection bring meaning to our lives?
6. Please read Hebrews 6:10–11. What does this passage speak to you?

Conclusion

Most of us are familiar with the *Christmas Story*—how Jesus was born to Mary the virgin in the small town of Bethlehem (Luke 2:1-20). Because there was no room elsewhere, Mary gave birth to Jesus in a barnlike structure, wrapped Him in cloths, and laid Him in a feeding trough. Glorious angels then announced Christ's birth—not to kings, priests, or wealthy merchants, but to lowly shepherds.

Many are also familiar with how the wicked King Herod ordered all male babies near Bethlehem murdered because he saw the Christ Child as a threat to his lineage (Matthew 2:1-18). Herod's evil plans led God to send the Magi home by another road.

Not nearly as many people, however, know that King Herod had built a palace-fortress called "Herodium" as a monument to himself, only about three miles from Bethlehem. An accomplished builder, Herod took a small hill and turned it into a mountain fortress using slaves, servants, and artisans. Within the complex, the Rome-appointed king enjoyed pools of freshly supplied water, beautiful gardens, and a luxurious palace. Jesus was born in humble surroundings, but within sight of the towering walls of Herod's luxurious version of paradise.

The contrast between Jesus and Herod broadcasts the good news of the kingdom like nothing else. While the human elite seek to elevate themselves at the expense of others, humble love characterizes the kingdom of God. As Mary herself proclaimed before Christ's birth:

> "He has done mighty deeds with His arm;
> He has scattered those who were proud in the thoughts of their heart.
> "He has brought down rulers from their thrones,
> And has exalted those who were humble."
> Luke 1:51-52

Herein lies our understanding of the good news of the kingdom: *everything about God's design is intended to bless humanity while eliminating the potential for self-centered pride.* Any form of religion that does not align with this design misses the mark, being birthed of human logic and not divine wisdom.

OUR RESPONSE

I would not be surprised if these ideas challenge your thinking the way they have my own. The essence of God's kingdom is not natural, so how can we grasp supernatural concepts without help from the Holy Spirit? Sure, some will try to make the kingdom about government laws, or social movements, or material wealth, but those efforts always miss the mark. I prefer to embrace the apostle Paul's description of the kingdom being about "righteousness and peace and joy in the Holy Spirit" (Romans 14:17).

It has been said that "the kingdom is here but not yet." I like that statement. The kingdom of God first came to earth through Jesus, the King of Glory. And with the Day of Pentecost, it began to spread, bringing light to the darkest corners of the globe. But the kingdom is not yet here in its fullness. That time will arrive when Jesus returns to earth—not as a suffering servant, but a victorious King. He will not come simply to lift the broken and downtrodden from an ash heap of misery, but to rescue His people and bring judgment upon the prideful hearts opposing His good rule. The idea of judgment might not appeal to the average mind, but it is necessary for all to be set in order.

On the Day of Judgment, we will not answer to a pastor, priest, or denominational leader, but to God Himself. So while we want to respect our religious authorities, we must always seek God's way first through the writings of the Bible. If we approach the Scriptures with sincere, honest, and humble hearts, the Lord will guide our paths.

Though our heavenly Father accepts us as we are and chooses to see us through the lens of Christ's righteousness, transforming our lives is high on His priority list. Through the process of sanctification, the Lord will use everything in our lives—including successes, failures, and relational conflicts—to grow us to *spiritual maturity* so we might mirror Christ through our character, attitudes, and actions.

Conclusion

FOLLOWING ABRAHAM'S FOOTSTEPS

The Bible paints a picture of Abraham (a.k.a. Abram) as the *father* of our Christian faith (Romans 4; Galatians 3:6-9). The Lord called Abraham out of the commonality and corruption of ancient idolatry with a *promise* of something greater:

> "Go out from your land,
> your relatives,
> and your father's house
> to the land that I will show you.
> I will make you into a great nation,
> I will bless you,
> I will make your name great,
> and you will be a blessing.
> I will bless those who bless you,
> I will curse those who treat you with contempt,
> and all the peoples on earth
> will be blessed through you."
> Genesis 12:1b-3 (HCSB)

Abraham's promise became a *journey*—one of sanctification. From the very beginning, the Lord intended to bless the man richly, but his life story reflects an ancient proverb:

> An inheritance gained hurriedly at the beginning
> Will not be blessed in the end.
> Proverbs 20:21

Abraham needed to grow into His calling, so his character could handle the weight of heavenly glory. Through many ups and downs, our spiritual forefather became the ultimate hero of transformational faith. And though the Lord blessed Abraham with wealth, land, and a rich lineage, God's covenant friend spied something greater in the distance. Hebrews 11:10 (HCSB) tells us "he was looking forward to the city that has foundations, whose architect and builder is God."

As the father of our faith, Abraham's life provides a *pattern* for all of us. Heaven's King is calling us to step out of our comfort zones—out of the commonality and corruption of an idolatrous world—to a glorious destiny we cannot quite see.

Like Abraham, ours is a journey that will challenge us to the core. Every weakness, shortcoming, and impurity will be laid bare—brought to the surface of our lives so we might be sanctified in the image of our Savior. If you begin to feel overwhelmed along the way, you can help minimize confusion by remembering Abraham's experience.

To begin, the Christian life is always to be lived by *faith* (Habakkuk 2:4). There will be times we need to shift our focus from encroaching rules and expectations to simply trusting God. The Lord is faithful to His promises no matter what our circumstances seem to say. And as with Abraham, His faithfulness will become more evident *after* we persevere through our trials (Romans 4:16–21).

Second, God promised *greatness* for Abraham, but such favor became realized in the man's call to *bless others*. The Lord will fulfill His plans for our lives as we selflessly serve the well-being of those around us. True greatness comes not from seeking greatness but from seeking to humbly bless others (Acts 20:35). And so it is that *love* fulfills the requirements of the law (Romans 13:8–10; Galatians 5:14).

Third, we need *wisdom* any time we step into the unknown from what is comfortable and familiar. Seek God's wisdom as you would hidden treasure, and He will guide your paths, while rewarding you with spiritual riches beyond measure (Proverbs 2:1–15).

Finally, entering into a covenant relationship with God means *the King of heaven has your back*. No matter how others treat you, the Lord's favor will establish and elevate you in the end (Ephesians 2:4–7).

TRAVELING TOGETHER

The new covenant path of sanctification is not meant to be trod alone; getting connected with a healthy local church is essential. We need *relationships* with devoted, godly, and mature Christians. Look for a mature believer to disciple you. Or involve yourself in a reputable small group Bible study. Or both. I consider it foolish to think we can become all God wants without being connected to Christ's body.

Conclusion

No doubt, there are many unhealthy churches in our world, but I also see the Lord at work in profound ways. When discouragement creeps into my view of the church, I go to Ephesians 5:25-27 and am reminded of God's plan to return *for a bride without spot or blemish*. Amid all the shortcomings and failures that seem to parade before us, our Savior continues to prepare a beautiful, victorious bride for His return. Some truly amazing people help form the body of Christ; we just need to find and align ourselves with them.

I still have questions regarding the Christian faith and how everything will play out at the end of our age. I think we all do. The core elements, however, can be settled with reasonable certainty. As long as we love truth more than human opinions—including our own—the Lord will disclose to us the wisdom of His kingdom. And the more I understand about God's good kingdom, the more I become enamored with His glorious plan. A thousand times over, I choose heaven's Monarch and the substance of His eternal kingdom—no matter what the cost. Nothing can compare.

But what about you? Will you embrace the Biblical Jesus, or cling to old mindsets and traditions? Will you repent of your pride? Will you humble your heart to ask forgiveness? Will you reach your arms toward the Savior and gain a depth of heavenly favor you could never earn for yourself? Will you fully surrender your will to the sovereign King of heaven and earth? Will you die to your self-will so God can use you to bring hope and life to others? Will you put off the old and put on the new? Will you let go of bitterness? Will you allow the Lord to instill your life with purpose? Will you be faithful to His calling? Will you yield so your Creator can sanctify you for His kingdom purposes? There is no time like now. And if not now, when?

No matter what we go through in devotion to our King, it will be worth it in the end. The kingdom of God will one day arrive in full, leaving every earthly kingdom in its wake. And, together, we will dine and rejoice in paradise at the marriage supper of the Lamb.

For now, by faith, we see that day in the distance. But it will not remain distant forever. The kingdom of heaven will soon become our ever-present reality. No matter how imposing the obstacles or intense the adversity, we will taste the euphoria of heaven's glorious kingdom as long as we persevere through the journey.

When the journey seems endless and its completion unattainable, we want to focus on living step by step. Every sunrise provides an opportunity to begin anew. The prophet Jeremiah reminds us that God's mercies are new every morning:

> Because of the Lord's faithful love
> we do not perish,
> for His mercies never end.
> They are new every morning;
> great is Your faithfulness!
> Lamentations 3:22-23 (HCSB)

Each day is a new beginning, a fresh start. You can fall fifty times and on the fifty-first you will overcome. I do not entirely understand the depths of our Savior's grace, but His patience is immeasurable, and He provides what we need for each step along the way.

There is a King—all-powerful, all-knowing, sovereign, eternal, good, and unselfish—whose kingdom is advancing across the globe. With each piece of ground gained, evil is vanquished and human lives restored. On a day yet to come, His kingdom will be the only one standing.

Acknowledgments

I want to say writing is always a joy, that every time I touch my keyboard I sense heaven's bliss. But I cannot. Certainly, there are times when I sense the Lord's pleasure and feel the Spirit's anointing, but writing a book also involves a lot of hard work. The tedious attention to detail can be especially challenging for someone with my short attention span.

The challenges of attempting to write well make me especially grateful for those who come alongside to help improve the quality of my work. I never cease to be amazed by how the Lord interweaves their unique contributions to my writing efforts.

Dave Clites, Deb Croyle, K-Lee Gaffney, Jack Hempfling, Jason Hutchins, Jackie Kuehn, Lynda Logue, Samantha Mitchell, Elaine Rice, Debi Santos, Paula Saylor, Mark Sterlace, Judah Thomas, and Phyllis Walls, I deeply appreciate all of you, along with the many others who help make our publishing efforts possible.

About the Author

Bob Santos writes to see lives transformed by God's goodness. Years of working in college ministry revealed that people crave to know more about God not only in their hearts through faith, but also through a deeper understanding of the truths found in His Word.

Pursuing spiritual vitality, Bob helps others "connect the dots" of Biblical truth by addressing "missing links" of contemporary theology. In this, Bob's books and video teachings explore key Biblical themes—such as covenants, grace, identity, rest, unity, and wisdom—that are often misunderstood or widely ignored. His explanations of difficult concepts, combined with inspirational messages of hope in Christ, are insightful, thought-provoking, and transformational as they explore the Christian faith in an understandable and yet intellectually satisfying way.

Bob was licensed for Christian ministry in 1997 and ordained in 2005 through Elim Fellowship (www.elimfellowship.org). In 2006, Bob and his wife Debi founded Search for Me Ministries, Inc. (sfme.org) with the mission to help form and equip a generation of world changers for Christ through the production of Biblically-based teaching resources.

College sweethearts, Bob and Debi have been married for over forty years. They have two adult children, two grandchildren, and three granddogs. When he is not writing, speaking, or leading a Bible study, you will likely find Bob doing something in the great outdoors.

Additional Resources from Search for Me Ministries

Additional copies of *The Good News of the Kingdom* can be purchased through major online retailers. Volume discounts are available through SfMe Ministries (sfme.org) for ministry organizations.

Deciding what to teach and preach about can present a significant challenge for pastors and ministry leaders. *The Teleios Trail: Thirty Topics to Explore for Spiritual Growth* is an excellent resource to help grow spiritually mature disciples of Christ.

Division has long plagued the church, reflecting badly on Christianity and hindering our mission. *Greater Glory: The Transformational Power of Christian Unity* challenges us to embrace God's perspective so we can live out the lifestyle of love that is central to our faith. (Audiobook available)

There is a profound logic behind all that God does, but it is not human logic. *The Age of Abiding: Experiencing the Life of the Vine* provides powerful insights into human nature, helping the reader better grasp the mysterious beauty of the Christian gospel. (Audiobook available)

The Search for Rest: Fifty Days to a More Peaceful Life provides an awesome personal or group study that explores the concept of the Sabbath from both spiritual and physical perspectives. This thought-provoking book meets a powerful need in a world that is filled with anxiety and unrest. (Audiobook available)

Much of the Christian faith makes little sense to the modern, Western mind because the Bible was written with a mentality that differs from current thought. *Drinking Truth: Embracing the Covenant Mindset of the Bible* provides an insightful look at the new covenant in light of the covenantal mindset with which the Bible was penned. (Audiobook available)

The *Community Prayer Devotional* is a powerful book that brings churches together to pray. Even better, the cover can be personalized to fit your community, allowing people to take ownership and embrace prayer as a lifestyle! (Audiobook available)

If you want to gain a Biblical perspective on identity, *From Glory to Glory: Finding Real Significance in an Image-Driven World* is the book for you! Not only is this powerful forty-day devotional filled with illuminating insights, it will also help to renew your mind as a beloved child of the King of Glory. (Audiobook available)

Say Goodbye to Regret: Discovering the Secret to a Blessed Life is a life-changing book that deals with the problem of regret on two fronts. Learn how to move beyond the lingering pain of regret and also how to avoid regrets entirely by pursuing the rich treasures of God's spiritual wisdom. (Audiobook available)

The TouchPoint: Connecting with God through the Bible is a valuable resource for those who are interested in learning more about the Bible. Revised in 2020, this book provides a great introduction to the Christian Scriptures while emphasizing a personal relationship with God. (Audiobook available)

The Divine Progression of Grace: Blazing a Trail to Fruitful Living thoughtfully explores God's grace from a perspective of empowerment as well as acceptance. This book will take you deeper into a relationship with your Creator and also help make you more usable for His purposes.

Each reading in *Champions in the Wilderness: Fifty-Two Devotions to Guide and Strengthen Emerging Overcomers* draws from a deep well of truth to encourage, strengthen, and instruct those who desire to walk with God but are struggling in the face of adversity. The format of this devotional lends itself well to group discussion. (Audiobook available)

Posting Book Reviews

Please consider posting an online review of this book. Honest reviews are deeply appreciated and provide an easy way for our readers to contribute to our ministry efforts. Also, if your life has been touched by one of our resources, please recommend it to others.

SfMe Media

SfMe Media belongs to Search for Me Ministries, Inc. (SfMe Ministries)—an IRS-recognized 501(c)(3) nonprofit organization. Search for Me Ministries burns with a vision to help form and equip a generation of world changers for Christ. We believe in the importance of reaching those who do not know the Lord, but we also recognize the need for healthy churches as landing places for new believers. By helping Christians grow to maturity with our uniquely flavored teaching resources, we are helping to create environments that foster the fulfillment of the Great Commission in every way.